Beneath the Steps:
A Writing Guide for 12-Step Recovery

Cover design:

Cindy Stewart

Cover photo

"Happy, joyous and free"
C. Beck

Beneath the Steps

A Writing Guide to 12 Step Recovery

Copyright © 2019 by Christine Beck

ISBN: 9781688936324

Flying Horse Press
West Haven, CT Tony Fusco

Beneath the Steps: A Writing Guide for 12-Step Recovery
by Christine Beck

Note to Reader

This book is designed for anyone in 12-step recovery. Its premise is simple: I have learned that creative writing aids recovery by connecting life experience with healing as we remove the obsession with alcohol (or other addictive substance) or with an alcoholic, past or present. This is particularly true if we were raised in an alcoholic or dysfunctional family. By writing about our story and sharing with others, we allow a Higher Power of creativity to enter our lives and make us whole.

This book weaves my story in three 12-step programs: Alcoholics Anonymous (AA), Al-Anon, and Adult Children of Alcoholics and Dysfunctional Families (ACA) with poems I have written. After each poem, I offer a "Prompt" to guide you in writing your own story. Since 2016, I have guided ten women in different 12-step recovery programs in writing and sharing their writing. You do not need to write to the Prompts in any order. You do not need to write poems. Just twenty minutes spent in any type of writing in response to the Prompts in this book will aid your recovery.

I got sober in 2006 in AA and began Al Anon recovery in 2008. I added ACA recovery in 2014. My father was an alcoholic. My mother was a Jehovah's Witness. I married an Adult Child of an Alcoholic or Dysfunctional Family, which we call an Adult Child. You will relate to some of my experiences and not others. I've learned in recovery to relate rather than compare and hope you will find benefit in these pages despite differences in our personal backgrounds. Where I use "she," think "me!"

Because our healing and understanding isn't linear, poetry can help us approach recovery sideways, using emotion, the senses and memory to sort through the layers. Poetry will help you uncover buried memories. Your Higher Power, working through your pen, will lead you to hope, healing and acceptance. You will discover your true self and live a life of deep purpose and serenity. I welcome you on this important journey.

poem, I offer a "Prompt" to guide you in writing your own story. Since 2016, I have guided ten women in different 12-step recovery programs in writing and sharing their writing. You do not need to write to the Prompts in any order. You do not need to write poems. Just twenty minutes spent in any type of writing in response to the Prompts in this book will aid your recovery.

I got sober in 2006 in AA and began Al Anon recovery in 2008. I added ACA recovery in 2014. My father was an alcoholic. My mother was a Jehovah's Witness. I married an Adult Child of an Alcoholic or Dysfunctional Family, which we call an Adult Child. You will relate to some of my experiences and not others. I've learned in recovery to relate rather than compare and hope you will find benefit in these pages despite differences in our personal backgrounds. Where I use "she," think "me!"

Because our healing and understanding isn't linear, poetry can help us approach recovery sideways, using emotion, the senses and memory to sort through the layers. Poetry will help you uncover buried memories. Your Higher Power, working through your pen, will lead you to hope, healing and acceptance. You will discover your true self and live a life of deep purpose and serenity. I welcome you on this important journey.

Table of Contents

Why Write for Recovery   1

Why Poetry?   3

How Writing Has Helped my Recovery   4

The Approach of this Book   7

TOPICS AND THE STEPS   8

WRITING ABOUT YOUR ALCOHOLISM
OR ADDICTION   10

    Talk Me Off the Ledge   11
    Kendall Jackson   13
    How to Stop Drinking   16
    If I Should Disappear   18
    Manhattan Tower   21
    Against the Odds   23
    Spirits   25
    Meet Me   27

WRITING ABOUT YOUR FAMILY HISTORY   28

Ancestors   28
    James Hardy & Harald Haraldson   29
    Scarf   32
    Yarn   34

Parents' Marriage   36
    Wedding Day   36

Family Secrets   38
    Gladys   39
    Grandfather Clock   41
    Two Figures in Search of a Story   43
    The Manicure   45

**WRITING ABOUT CHILDHOOD LOSSES
OR WOUNDS**   47

I Don't Remember   49

Childhood experience of death   51
Baby Boy   52

Shame of Alcoholic Parent
Future Entrepreneurs   56

Sunday Dinner   58

Violence and feeling unsafe   60
Walking Home

Abandonment   62
Stood Up   63
Can Anybody Hear Me?   65
Musical Chairs   67

Feeling Not Good Enough   69
Shame on You   69
Privilege   71
Cattywampus   73
Ahab   75
Objects   77

Sexual abuse and sexual confusion   78
Safe House   79
First Kiss   80
Batting Practice   82

Break-up of family of origin
Starting Over   84
Brearley House   86

Losing Friends 87

    Easter at the Cemetery 87

    Zest 89

Religious Abuse 91

    Converted 91

    Dot 93

    Five Corners 96

    The End of Santa 98

    We Must Have Prayed

        for Something 101

Death of Parents 102

    John Doe 43 102

    What's Left 105

    Funeral Instructions 106

    Given Salt, Given Time 108

    What I Never Wanted 110

RETRIEVING HAPPY CHILDHOOD

MEMORIES 111

    What's Inside 111

    Love of the Four Legged 113

    Outside the Frame 115

    Spencer Iowa 117

    Melodies 119

CONNECTING CHILDHOOD WOUNDS TO

CHARACTER TRAITS 120

Fear of Abandonment 122

    Taking out the Trash 123

    Mother-in-law 125

    Katie Gibbs School 1965 126

Shame 128

    Legacy 129

    Squirm 130

People Pleasing 131

    My Daughter's Birthday 132

    The Scent of Fear 133

Losing Our Identity 135

    City Lights, San Francisco 135

    Stand Up 137

    If Feelings Could Talk 139

    Boundaries 141

    Born to Run 143

    Living in the Projects 146

Denial 147

    Denial 148

Using Sex to Manipulate/Avoid

    Being Abandoned 149

    The Contenders 150

    Bridalveil Falls 151

    Under Spanish Skies 154

    What I Would Say to Monica

        Lewinsky 157

    Ashes of Dead Lovers 159

Fear of Anger and Chaos 160

    Manifesto of the Sick and Tired 160

Being Rescuers 161

    The Rescuer 162

    Rescue Me 163

Acting as Victims 165

    In the Land of Victimhood 166

Confusing Love and Pity 168

    I'd Never Met a Vet 168

    The Dailies 170

Attraction to Dysfunctional People   172

   Watching Walter Cronkite   172

   Sometimes He Comes Home

      Bloody   174

   Secondhand Smoke   176

FINDING A HIGHER POWER   178

   Envisioning Your Higher Power   179

   Night's Blessing   180

   Comforter   181

   Animals as a Spiritual Experience   182

   Eye Contact   183

   Music Can Invite a Higher Power   184

   I Owe It All To You   185

   Children as a Spiritual Experience   186

   Swans and Hearts   187

   Portrait in Elizabeth Park   189

   Morning Song   191

   Nature as a Spiritual Experience   192

   Revelation   193

   Valley of Shadows   195

   Places Where You Have Had a Spiritual

   Experience   196

   Here and There   197

   Visible   200

   Being "Good Enough"   202

   The Wading Pool   202

   Prayer and Meditation   203

   Meditation from my Front Step   204

   Why Am I Here?   205

   Take It   207

   Monk, Mountainside, Meditation   210

MAKING AMENDS 213
    Happy Spring 213

Writing about Forgiveness
    Sorry/Not Sorry 215

Amends to Ourselves 216
    My Bad 216
    Beneath Your Smile 219

People We Have Manipulated 220
What is Your Emergency? 221

Our Parents 223
    Restore Us 224

Our Partner or Spouse 225
    Reasons 226

Our Children 227
    What Goes Around 228

Failed Relationships 229
    Joyce 230
    What About Bob? 232

People in Authority we Defied 234
    The Dean 234
    Quitting Time 236

REPARENTING YOUR INNER CHILD 238
Identifying the Voice of the Inner
Critical Parent 238
    You Should Have Known Better 238

Finding the Voice of an Inner
Loving Parent 240
    My Inner Loving Parent Speaks 242

Listening to Your Inner Child   245

    Home   246

    Tinoskaya   247

    Offerings   249

FINDING YOUR TRUE SELF   252

    From the Washtub, 1948   252

    Who Am I?   253

    Googling Myself   255

    Can You See Me Now?   257

LEARNING HOW TO PLAY AND HAVE FUN   260

    Jumping for Joy   260

FINDING SERENITY, PEACE AND LOVE   263

    Field Service   263

    Flying with the Man Who Looks
       at Nothing   265

WRITING YOUR WAY INTO YOUR FUTURE   267

    Gone Gently   267

A BLESSING   269

Why Write for Recovery

Twelve-Step recovery work frequently uncovers trauma or wounds from childhood as well as fears and uncomfortable feelings. Denial, once our friend and protector, turns against us as memories resurface. Healing a trauma or wound requires that we talk about it, yet that is usually the last thing we want to do. We want to put it behind us, forget about it, move on. And those around us frequently want the same thing. They don't want us to relive pain and they don't want to relive it with us.

Yet I have discovered that writing makes the most difference to my recovery when I feel that I am taking a painful experience and reforming it, turning it into something that seems useful, something others might experience as providing an opening to step into. I also frequently surprise myself in my writing. Something I didn't know I knew reveals itself.

Many of us have been advised to write daily in a journal to help heal a grief or wound. I don't discount journaling, but for me, it often turns into either a diary of what is happening in my life, a list of grievances or complaints, or a list of resolutions about changing some behavior. Without guidance on what to write about, my writing doesn't seem to relate to recovery.

The tools of poetry have been instrumental in my recovery. Poetry uses images, sound, repetition, and rhythm to create an emotional experience on the page. The poem may tell a story or it may describe a scene or feeling. But underlying most poetry is generally a strong emotion. Wordsworth said that poetry is "the spontaneous overflow of powerful emotion . . . recollected in tranquility." The writer, and by extension the reader, enters into the poem by connecting with images and with words that touch the reader through sound, rhythm, musicality, or their unexpectedness that stirs up the reader to recognize something powerful.

But here is the important part for writers in recovery. That same experience the writer hopes to evoke in the reader is first revealed to

1

the writer in the process of writing. That is, the writer doesn't start off with a "mission" to convey some basic truth or emotional experience to the reader. The writer may have no idea what he is feeling or thinking. But in the process of putting words on paper, they discover something new. The first "discovery" is the writer's. That the words may touch the reader is a wonderful and sacred experience. But this book is about YOU, the writer. It is about discovering experiences that you have forgotten, reclaiming those experiences, and discovering the healing that can only occur when you connect the experience with the feeling.

One of the most powerful survival traits in people working a recovery program is denial. We begin to recognize our level of denial slowly. Experiences and feelings we have denied return on a timetable that may seem excruciatingly slow. I believe denial is what helped many of us survive. We can thank our denial and treat it as a powerful invisibility cloak that protected us for years. But in recovery we come to see that our invisibility cloak keeps us isolated from other people. It worked as a mask of "good, good, everything's fine." As we slowly come to realize that everything was not really so good, and even today, things may not be so fine, we create openings for recovery.

Many of us fear that without our invisibility cloak, there will be nothing within to reclaim. "Who am I? What do I want to be when I grow up? How do I figure that out?" We people-pleasers have spent years trying to meet everyone else's wants and needs so we won't be physically or emotionally abandoned. We may not have any idea what our own wants and needs are. I guarantee that you will get in touch with your wants and needs through the process of writing. It's not a six-month guarantee. I've been doing it for many years. But I do guarantee that if you keep at it, you will come to know what you need to know to live a happy and contented life. It's already inside you. It's simply been inaccessible as a result of your survival traits.

In writing, you will discover that there is no one "right way" of discovering and expressing your spirit. That is the beauty of your being unique. But in connecting deeply felt longings and fears to "image" and "story," you will learn to reveal your True Self. You will reclaim a sense of authenticity and purpose. You will be able to give and accept love in healthy relationships.

How, then, can you turn your experience into creative writing? I suggest writing in response to the writing of others who are on a similar journey and letting your Higher Power take over your pen. Think of yourself as a scribe and your Higher Power as the creator of the words. What is this "Higher Power?" Many in recovery call it God, but almost all writers acknowledge a creative power. You can think of it as a muse, as a power of openness and wonder, or as a power that allows you to "open the door" in your writing.

Why Poetry?

Poetry is designed to uncover mystery. In writing an essay, for example, I research, outline, and develop a list of points to make. The creative writer does the opposite. The poet isn't a rhetorician in this respect. We hold the pen lightly, trusting that by stirring up the unconscious and focusing on an image, a speech pattern, or a snippet of language, something remarkable will result. That doesn't mean that all poems written this way will reveal a hidden truth. Sometimes, writing feels like a dead-end. A writer's drawers are full of what may at first seem like failed drafts. But we can often retrieve them, or parts of them, at a later date, when we see the connection between the original impulse and where the poem needs to "go" to do its work.

Poetry is my chosen form of writing. I know many people have an automatic negative reaction to the word "poetry." Let me dispel that concern. This book contains suggestions for what I call a "free-write," which means to write in response to a "Prompt" in any form that feels right to you. Your free-write may lead to a poem, a short story, a novel, a memoir, or simply a fragment to help you discover something important for your recovery. The final "form" is not important. It is "the work" that heals us.

Why do I choose poetry? First, poetry connects me to my Inner Child. The Inner Child is a term used in ACA. It is the part of us that is "stuck" emotionally in a childhood state where we felt abandoned, not important, or abused in some way. If this term strikes you as odd, just "hold that thought." It took me years in ACA recovery before I was willing to acknowledge an Inner Child. One way to connect with your Inner Child is to recall poems and songs from a young age, before you began to build your defenses. One of my favorite poems is by Robert Louis Stevenson, which begins:

The Swing

How do you like to go up in a swing
Up in the air so blue?
Oh, I do think it the pleasantest thing
Ever a child can do. . .

This poem uses rhythm, rhyme and repetition, all delightful tools in poetry. These all create pleasure and embed in memory.

Also, poetry lets me distill a scene, story, image or emotion on one page. I am a "sucker for cheap closure," too impatient to wait ten or twenty pages to get to "the good part."

If you want to learn more about the craft of poetry, see the Appendix where I list Poetic Terms and how to use them.

How Writing Has Helped my Recovery

I started writing poetry in the year 2000 after a twenty-year career as a lawyer ended. I didn't want to write a poem. It was an "assignment" from a therapist. (The poet Anne Sexton also wrote her first poem at a therapist's instruction, so I feel I'm in good company.) He said to take an image from a dream and write a poem about it. "No," I said. "I don't like poetry." He said, "Do it anyway." As I was paying good money for his advice and didn't have any better ideas, I did what he asked. I wrote about a dream in which I was grilling fish in the ocean. The poem turned into one about going fishing with my dad. My early poems were angry and filled with self-pity. A friend read them and said, "You are really angry with your father!" I didn't see them that way, (I thought I was just telling the truth) but I'm sure she was right. That's where I had to begin.

My father was an alcoholic. I became one too. Today I know that alcoholism is a family disease. I began my program of recovery from alcoholism after I turned fifty-five. My "sobriety date" is February 22, 2006. The following year, I began an Al Anon program. Eight years after that, I began recovery in the Adult Children of Alcoholics and Dysfunctional Families program (called ACA).

I summarize my experience of the three programs this way. AA taught me that alcohol was not my "problem." It was my solution. In order to stop drinking, I had to accept the need for help from a Higher Power, even if that Higher Power was only the AA group. I had to learn to accept people, places and things as they are in order to know peace. And I had to examine my own causes and conditions that led to the need for the relief that alcohol provided.

Al Anon taught me that I can obsess about an alcoholic—one in my life today or one from my past. I must learn to detach with love from the other people in my life. I do not need to accept unacceptable behavior. I can set boundaries about how and where I will interact with alcoholics in my life. But I am responsible for my own happiness, and I can be happy whether the alcoholic is drinking or not.

The ACA program taught me that growing up in an alcoholic or dysfunctional family results in shared characteristics, such as fear of abandonment, the need to control, codependence (focusing on others' wants and needs rather than one's own) and overwhelming feelings of shame. Many of these survival traits are the same as what A.A calls "character defects." But ACA reminds me that these traits affect everyone raised the way I was. I did nothing wrong. I couldn't have turned out any other way. This relieves me of shame. The purpose of ACA is to teach me how to notice triggers in daily life that cause me to react based on fear and how to recognize, and care gently for, a valuable and lovable Inner Child within me.

All three programs use the same "12 steps" of recovery originally developed by AA. At the heart of all 12-step programs is an acknowledgement that we are powerless. As children, we were literally powerless over our caretakers. When one or more of them is an alcoholic or otherwise dysfunctional, the powerlessness becomes fear—fear of abandonment and fear for our physical safety. This results in an adult who is imprisoned in childhood reactions.

An Al Anon who obsesses about getting an alcoholic sober is also powerless. Thoughts such as "if you really loved me, you would stop drinking," or "where is your will power?" demonstrate how such powerlessness can become a trap.

The alcoholic feels powerless over the first drink, and once consumed, powerless over how many they will drink or the consequences of getting drunk. The craving or obsession for a drink is usually an obsession to change the way we feel. We think alcohol will bring a sense of ease and comfort that seems lacking in our lives. But with us, the ease and comfort of the first drink quickly becomes the self-hatred and remorse of getting drunk, blacking out, and acting out.

The stories you will write are not lists of people we resent, or the "drunkalogues" of bad behavior that can become tedious in AA. They are the stories of how we became people who felt that we did not fit in, isolated, lonely, people-pleasers or angry and judgmental. The seeds are there in our stories.

The Approach of this Book

I will show you some poems and then pose a series of questions (called "Prompts") to guide your writing in response. My poems reveal my personal story. Yours will be different. My father was an alcoholic. I became one too. Drugs are not a part of my story, but the obsessive thinking and the desire to change the way we feel apply to drugs as well as alcohol. I did not have a mentally ill parent or one afflicted with another addiction, such as gambling. I know that the language of this book, which is the language of 12-step recovery, applies to all of us, regardless of gender, age, or the nature of our addiction or the addiction or dysfunction (other substances, food, people, gambling, sex and love, work, etc. or other compulsions) we grew up in. Also, while I use "alcohol" and "alcoholic" as a shorthand in this book, alcoholism is not the only family type that leads to growing up with addictions, compulsions, codependence, etc. Children who grow up in such dysfunction often arrive at adulthood with the same fear, shame and low self-esteem.

I invite you to replace the word "alcoholic" with "addict, gambler, dysfunctional caretaker, codependent, compulsive personality, mentally ill" etc. as needed to relate to your family background and current situation.

Once we realize that alcoholism is a family disease that affected our parents, grandparents, and ancestors, we can connect what we know of their stories to our own lives and struggles. We were literally powerless over our parents' and grandparents' lives before we were born. But writing about them helps us uncover the trauma that we hold in our DNA and that permeates our bodies. This is often called post-traumatic stress. While it may seem odd that we can hold PTS from events that occurred long before we were born, this concept has been recognized by the Greeks and in the Bible. Although we may not believe that the "sins of the fathers are visited upon the sons," there is an important kernel of truth to this idea, one we can connect with in writing.

Topics and the Steps

The poetry and prompts are organized around the following recovery steps/topics:

Your Alcoholism or other Primary Compulsive Addiction

This topic corresponds to step 1 (powerlessness.)

Writing about Your Family's History; Losses and Wounds from Your Childhood

These topics correspond roughly to Step 4 (inventory)

Character Traits that Impede Your Recovery

This topic corresponds to steps 5 and 6, in which we list our character traits and work to remove them. Uncovering our character traits takes time and patience. This is because we come into recovery in denial about our part in broken relationships. The ACA program has a list of 14 of these traits, which is an excellent starting point.

Finding a Higher Power.

This corresponds to steps 2 (came to believe) 3 (surrendered to a Higher Power) and 11 (prayer and meditation).

This is a component of all twelve-step recovery. We need to move out of isolation, the denial that we do not need help, and learn to trust. Some view a Higher Power as the recovery group itself. Some connect with a more traditional "God." But we all agree that relying on our own power doomed us to repeat our addictions. Somehow, we must find a power greater than ourselves.

Making Amends.

This corresponds to steps 8 (list people we have harmed) and 9 (made amends.) The AA program focuses first on amends that result from bad behavior while drinking. However, amends based on acting out on character traits is even more important. We need to become aware of them before we can take any action to change them.

Reparenting your Inner Child; Finding your True Self.

These topics correspond to the "promises" in all the programs.

The concept of an Inner Child, an Inner Loving Parent, and learning to "Reparent" our Inner Child is unique to ACA. However, AA stresses finding a true self in the slogan, "to thine own self be true," and Al Anon advises to focus on ourselves, rather than the alcoholic. ACA goes one step further with a process to discover and connect with our Inner Child, who is afraid and feels hurt. Although this may sound odd, we heal by telling ourselves those loving affirmations we did not hear in childhood until we believe and integrate them into our whole self. By recognizing that Inner Child and teaching the child to trust us, we gradually move out of denial and into healing. We are able to transform the traits that helped us survive childhood into healthy behavior.

When we are triggered today into acting out on our Character Traits, our Inner Child is often the one who is responding with fear. By Reparenting the Inner Child, we address the fear, reminding the child that we will not abandon the child, that we want to listen and help him or her respond in healthy ways. This is how we grow into our True Self.

Some people in ACA refer to the Inner Loving Parent as a Higher Power. Connecting with the spiritual tools of recovery and a loving Higher Power, including meditation and prayer help us reparent the Inner Child.

WRITING ABOUT YOUR ALCOHOLISM OR OTHER COMPULSIVE ADDICTION

In recovery, we meet many people like us who grew up with alcoholic, addicted or dysfunctional parents and swore they would never become like them. And we certainly wouldn't marry one. Yet many of us did both. There may be a genetic component to alcoholism that we may inherit from our parents. But why do children who grow up in an alcoholic household seem attracted to alcoholics? The answer is that we crave excitement and chaos because it is familiar and it makes us feel alive. We got used to trying to rescue and help the alcoholic parent. In adulthood, we often look for a partner we can treat the same way. It makes no "sense" to recreate a past many of us wished to escape. But we feel compelled to do so. Then we drink or practice some other addictive or compulsive behavior to numb the pain that results.

For years, I drank a couple of glasses of wine after work and during dinner. I didn't consider my drinking a "problem," but I drank every day. Looking back, I was always sure to have a supply of wine on hand. One night in college, when I ran out, I drank straight rum by myself out of a jelly glass in the kitchen, which should have been a tip-off that I had an alcohol problem. But even then, drinking was not really my problem. It was my solution to anxiety and fear.

Things got worse when I was fifty and took a teaching job at night. I'd come home at 10 pm to a sleeping house, but I was still keyed up from the adrenalin of teaching. What better way to relax than have a glass of wine? Prior to that job, I didn't drink after dinner. There were baths, bedtime stories, homework to check. I was too busy to drink.

I gave myself permission to drink alone. My two drinks a night turned into four. I decided to cut back. I used all the methods that sound silly once we learn that "you take a drink, and your drink takes a drink." It didn't matter what type of alcohol I switched to, or whatever other "controls" I put on my drinking. Once I drank one glass of wine, I had to have more. And for me, the more became too many.

10

Every time I drank, I didn't get in trouble. But many of my most embarrassing incidents involved alcohol. The time I sat on the senior partner's lap at our law firm outing at his country club? I was drunk. Some people laughed. I'm sure some were appalled. I was lucky I didn't tarnish my reputation and ruin my chances of advancement at the firm. The time another partner pushed into my hotel room on a business trip and refused to leave? We'd been drinking martinis. He kept repeating "But you held my hand," as we lurched up the steep streets in San Francisco. Actually, the martinis were holding his hand, but that was far too esoteric a debate. I told him I was going to stand outside in the hall until he left and that he would be really embarrassed the next morning. I did. He was.

What Led to Our Drinking or Addiction

Many of us drink to find ease and comfort. We feel awkward, uncomfortable, sometimes irritable and discontent. Yet ease and comfort is primarily a state of mind, not a state of body. As we explore these ideas, we can find ways to change our thoughts and behavior without alcohol. In the following poem, I write about a sense of ease and comfort that I long for.

Talk me off the Ledge

Show me the gift of violets,
their iridescent trembling stems,
clutched in my hand when I was ten
and gifts were free as grace.

Replay the meadows high above Yosemite,
tadpoles teeming in a mountain crater,
our angles zipped together in a deep
green sleeping bag.

Or sailing in the San Francisco bay,
dozing on the deck on a silver Monday
morning, work a distant window shining
on the fourteenth floor of commerce.

11

Remind me when I paddled in life's brew
like a tadpole, not knowing I'd outgrow my tail,
outlive my kin, bulge up in odd places.
Take my hand. Talk me off the ledge.

CONNECTION TO RECOVERY

In this poem, the "ledge" symbolizes the desire to drink. I remind myself that I have always been motivated by a desire to change the way I feel. The person talking me off the ledge is the voice of recovery.

PROMPT:

1.Write about the words "Ease and Comfort." Put yourself somewhere where you felt at ease without drinking.

2.Add someone you love to the scene and write a dialogue between the two of you. See what happens.

3.Write a "talk me off the ledge" poem in which someone you love tries to talk you into getting sober.

The following poem is written in a stream-of-consciousness fashion. I don't recall a lot after the second glass of wine on this flight to London, but I imagine the drunken monologue that can seem normal to an alcoholic mind:

Kendall Jackson

Here's the chardonnay, which I deserve, I do. It's Kendall Jackson, my favorite, not too expensive but with that kick of oak I yearn for. It's free here in business class, flying to London with my best friend Susan, aptly named I now see, Susan Jackson.

I don't remember much after the second glass, except it was so crisp and cool, a dance through the undergrowth of murky light, the shadows cast improbably from shafts of arrows poised all around me. It led me to still waters, a pond around the bend, blue, no slimy bottom, no leeches that attach to tender shins, impossible to touch, disgusting. And it's only two feet deep, the bottom clearly visible. I like to see the bottom, like the clarity of this chardonnay in its crystal wineglass.

I love its silky golden color, not too brazen, just the color I've been striving for all these years in a hair color. Natural, bright with depth in places. And the pond is surrounded by wildflowers, no more than one foot high. Surely no enemy could hide in Queen Anne's Lace, Cornflowers, or Black-eyed Susan's.   Why aren't cornflowers yellow, like corn? I've always wondered about that. Although I like the blue. I do.

Wildflowers speak to me, with their tender little centers, curled, inviting bees. So bucolic. Their stems are uncertain, they wave back and forth, pliable, and they are free for the picking, no rules with wildflowers. And here, amazingly, are the Susan's, my childhood friends. How could our mothers, who never met, name all three of us the same? We wear matching bathing suits, alike with our flat chests, our filly legs and close permed curls.

13

The suits are checkered pink and white, two pieces with a one- inch strip of untouched midriff. Oh, the purity of that skin, I miss it, as soft as newborns fuzz of golden hair so slight it gathers and reflects the sunlight, rather like this chardonnay, now I come to think of it. Kendall Jackson.

And then my grandparents, buried in Kendalville, Indiana, a farming town. A place I'd never been except for funerals and doubtless will never see again. A funeral with relatives who welcomed me as if they had always known me, although they'd never been to London and had no children named Susan. And my mother, dead at fifty, when I had yet to learn the saving grace of tears. I'd scurried back to work, refused a leave, stoic at her funeral. But I found geraniums in January, because that was what she asked for in her funeral instructions, and I was dutiful, I took my flowers seriously.

CONNECTION TO RECOVERY

The poem shows the crazy thinking that can accompany getting drunk. Some of it may seem funny, but underneath is an awareness of lost friends, dead relatives, and a girl who tried to give her mother the kind of flowers she wanted for her funeral.

Like most alcoholics, I tried to talk myself out of the obvious fact that I was drinking more and more. Then I switched what I drank to expensive wine, thinking financial considerations would help me cut back. I even enrolled in a study at a hospital that involved taking a pill and counting drinks. Everything failed. The following poem is called a "container poem." In the format of a "how to" article you might find on the internet, I wrote about How to Stop Drinking.

How to Stop Drinking

No point in telling yourself that Chardonnay tastes like Windex. It doesn't. It tastes like walking under waterfalls, like sinking backwards into bed with the guy you flirted with at the bar. It smells like a necklace made of daisy chains or the waft of Queen Anne's lace on a summer Sunday. It always has. It always will. Even the fourth or fifth glass (and that, of course is the problem) tastes just as good as the first.

Don't try aversion therapy. Even if they showed you livers corroded into cardboard, like those stone-black lungs of tiny Chinese men splayed open in an exhibit called "Bodies Revealed," you wouldn't stop. Face it, some smokers don't get lung cancer. Some drinkers have livers pink as kittens' tongues. You know that will be you. The one that gets away with it.

You didn't get caught—no DWI, no blackout at the kids' concert. You think of Robert Haas' poem "Dragonflies Mating" where his mother comes to his basketball practice, weaving across the gym, lipstick smeared, reeking, and he admits: "I wanted to kill her." No one wants to kill you.

Your kid comes home and tells you: "Mom, we learned in school today that anyone who drinks every day is an alcoholic." "No sweetie," you say, as you lift your Waterford crystal glass of Montrachet, "it's not people like us they meant. Of course we're not alcoholics."

But you know, don't you? You know where this is headed because you grew up at the feet of "just how bad it gets." Lift your gaze from the elixir swirling in your glass and take a look at what comes next.

This poem is a version of "thinking through the drink." It is filled with denial, but it ultimately turns to truth. We know where our addictions are heading. I knew when I entered recovery that I didn't want to be a drunk grandmother who could not be trusted to babysit. Nor did I want to be the drunk mother-of-the-bride, dancing with hips grinding and skirts flaring at my daughter's wedding. Those imaginary disasters help keep me sober.

PROMPT:

1.Write a "how to stop" poem about any behavior you would like to change. It could be drinking, eating, shopping, even obsessive thinking.

2.Start writing about all the ways it could have been worse. Then "turn" your poem to just how bad it got, or to a "yet," where it could go if left untreated.

I love fancy, romantic names of small wineries. They remind me of plazas in Europe and cheery red umbrellas. I've been told not to romanticize that which will kill me. The following poem is based on a true story of a murder that happened in Connecticut in which the accused husband claimed his wife had left him to escape her life. The scene at the end is my fantasy about escaping to drinking at a bar.

If I Should Disappear…
                    I.
Helle Crafts, a Swedish flight attendant,
told all her friends: If I should disappear,
don't think it's an accident. Don't believe
I flew home to Sweden or took off with a pilot

to start again in Barcelona. I'd never leave my girls
with Richard Crafts. Death splashed in the news:
murdered, stuffed in her freezer, then pulverized
like kindling in a chipper,

raining bits of body in the murky water
of the Housatonic. Her only trace: a tooth,
some strands of long blond hair, a fragment
of a bright red fingernail.
                    II.
As I stare at February's dirty snow, knowing
I am going nowhere, I tell my precious daughters,
whom I would never leave, and my husband,
who probably won't murder me:

If I should disappear, don't think it's an accident.
I'll be in Barcelona, flirting at a tapas bar,
on my 5th Cinzano, dangling a high-heeled sandal,
nibbling olives, savoring the salt.

CONNECTION TO RECOVERY

Here I link drinking with the death of Helle Crafts. This poem also illustrates the dangers of what is called a "geographic cure." If I think my disease will not come with me on vacation to Barcelona, I'm kidding myself.

Music can also stir longings to change the way I feel. I recall sitting on my bedroom floor playing records on a child's record player. My grandfather had a friend who owned a diner. When he replaced the records in his jukebox, he gave the outdated records to my grandfather, who gave them to me. I have long used scraps of song lyrics in creative writing. They seemed to float up out of memory.

One album I listened to over and over was the score of a musical called "Manhattan Tower," written by Gordon Jenkins in the 1940s. It was part of the jukebox rejects. The song was about a cocktail party: "Empty the ashtrays, Get out some ice/Cause, we're having a party, and the people are nice." The bartender's name was Noah. These lyrics even now remind me of my longing for cocktail parties and sophisticated conversation, where everyone was polite and no one started fights. For years, I remembered only this snippet of song. Then one day, the name Gordon Jenkins bubbled up. I found the album in 2010, over fifty years after I had obsessively memorized the lines. More remarkably, I rediscovered another track I'd forgotten, but probably listened to just as frequently: "Never Leave Me." Its refrain was: "Never leave me, never leave me/My heart is in your hands." There it was, the banner anthem for a child of an alcoholic, terrified of abandonment!

Deeply imbedded in our subconscious are words, images, lyrics and stories that connect us to our childhood, to pain, hurt, love and loss. If our free-writes begin with these specifics, they can lead us to important truths. Sometimes, patience is required, as with "Manhattan Tower."

Even as a young girl, I mixed the thought of alcohol and codependence: give me a drink and never leave me. The star of the musical, Steven, loses his love, Julie, at the end—a fact I had forgotten in the intervening fifty years. Why did a not-happily-ever-after musical so attract me? Perhaps it foreshadowed my parents breaking up, which in fact occurred when I was thirteen.

I combined some of the lyrics from Manhattan Tower in a poetic form called a pantoum, a repeating form. A pantoum echoes the physical description of dropping the needle on the record player and watching the record go around and around. I explain the form below. I planned the song lines to repeat, but the line about "caught half-naked in the bushes" and "someone else's wife" bubbled up into the poem unexpectedly. For me, they reveal the underside of getting drunk, a hook-up with someone else's wife. It makes the line "never leave me" even more poignant because someone has already "left" in an important way. Infidelity, real or imagined, was apparently one of my childhood fears or experiences.

Manhattan Tower

Empty the ashtrays, get out some ice
Ice, tinkling in the highball glass
Smoke from Luckies drifting
Cause we're having a party

Ice, tinkling in the highball glass
And the people are nice, nice
Cause we're having a party
Couples close enough to--

And the people are nice, nice
Caught half-naked in the bushes
Couples close enough to--
Luckies, Dewars, someone else's wife

Caught half-naked in the bushes
Never leave me, never leave me
Luckies, Dewars, someone else's wife
My heart is in your empty hands

Never leave me, never leave me
We're having a party, drifting
My heart is in your empty hands
Empty the ashtrays, get out some ice

CONNECTION TO RECOVERY

Music is embedded deep in our psyches, particularly music from our childhood. The magic land of Manhattan seemed to me the epitome of sophistication. Cocktail parties with fancy clothes, the clink of ice cubes, swish of satin skirts, and intellectual conversation struck a chord of deep longing. My family listened to Dick and Dorothy Kilgallen's radio show over the breakfast table. We existed on a defunct farm, while they were in Manhattan, relishing last night's party conversation. I didn't know the word for irony, but I know it now. Round and round the record went, building an image of a fantasy life.

PROMPT:

1.Write about your earliest memories of what "having a good time" meant to you. Try to connect it with a place, an event, or a person.

2.Repeat lines to show how that image embedded in you as something you would later long for.

3.Write the lyrics of songs you recall from childhood or adolescence. Don't think about them. Mix up lyrics or words. Then pick one of two and knit them together in an unexpected way.

4.Experiment with a repeating form, as emotions repeat in our lives and continue to repeat generations later. You can use a repeating form such as the pantoum. A pantoum is a poem of 4-line stanzas (quatrains) where lines 2 and 4 of the first verse are repeated as lines 1 and 3 of the following verse. Often, the poem ends repeating line 1.

I first started drinking in bars in Manhattan when I was 18, imagining the bars would lead to those dreamed-of cocktail parties. That didn't happen.

Against the Odds

Sunday mornings were devoted to The New York Times.
On Saturdays at midnight, I'd buy mine at the corner
of 64th and Lex, with change scrounged from my purse,
tuck it on the front hall table to read through Sunday noon.

The drinking age was eighteen, a bar on every corner.
Stingers were my drink of choice, a minty hit
of crème de menthe and brandy, as good as Crest,
without the need to spit.

First, The Lexington Café.
Then on to Carlow's, J. G. Melon's.
The East End Grill.
Then Barnaby's.

I was a horseman's daughter, knew not to bet against
the odds. But at O'Flanagan's, a maybe cute guy
one stool over said, I'll bet I can get you into bed by midnight.

The stingers took him on.

Midnight. I left him passed out on his Murphy bed
in Brooklyn, crept down four flights,
scrounging for the change to take a cab.

CONNECTION TO RECOVERY

This memory is one of my ten most humiliating moments. I'd like to say my good sense was simply overwhelmed by alcohol, but I made the bet when sober. "Drinking the guys under the table" sounded like a game I could win, a way of showing how cool I was, how well I could handle my liquor. I was so eager to get out of his apartment, I left my coat, a pretty bright green and navy color-blocked coat I'd made. The guy called me, asking to return it. I didn't see him or the coat again. A good, if quirky, reminder, of "keeping it green." This is Step 1 in the 12 steps of recovery. I thought I was in control, but I was powerless.

PROMPT:

1.Think about situations where you were drinking and should have said NO but didn't. What happened? What explanation did you use to make this conduct acceptable?

2.Write about any time you tried to make a point with your drinking, to show you were tough or worldly or sophisticated. Write about what you really felt inside.

My father drank cheap port wine. I upped the game and went for fancy Chardonnay. The effect, however, was the same. I stopped before I passed out, but I couldn't stop until I had drunk more than I wanted to, until I'd lost control and was at risk of making a fool of myself. The fear of embarrassing my children was a huge motivator in my getting sober. I have my father to thank for that. The following poem uses the labels on Chardonnays to explore the seduction of alcohol.

Spirits

At first, they helped: Turning Leaf, Wishing
Tree, Badger Mountain, Ravenswood,
Barefoot Cellars, Lost Horizons, Kissing Bridge,
Black Swan, Oasis Dogwood, Blackjack Ranch --
wines you could get lost in.

I'd hold a mouthful, let it wander over tongue
and teeth, splash like tender rainfall
in the Amazon, a warm enfolding mist,
invitation to peer up at a slip of sun.

Drain the glass, wine too dear to waste,
besides the glass holds precious little.
The waiter at my elbow sees it empty,
my subtle nod, "yes, please."

It doesn't hear the rage, ignores the fender
dents, bill collector battles. It's just as fun
drunk from the bottle, its gorgeous heft and sheen.

Then, discarded with the crumpled napkins,
stained linen, the bottle turns--
begins to eye the blonde across the room.

CONNECTION TO RECOVERY

This poem illustrates the power of marketing—how names on wine labels, TV with romantic scenes of drinking, images of parties from the past, can seduce me into alcoholic thinking. I admit my willingness when I say to the waiter, "yes, please," so polite, when there is nothing polite about being a drunk. The poem personifies alcohol as an evil force that traps me into ignoring the obligations of daily living. Ultimately, alcohol "turns" on me, as the bottle turns to the "blonde across the room."

PROMPT:

1. Write a poem about all the things you loved about drinking. Indulge in romanticism, the sense of ease and comfort it brought. Think of other activities you love and what is attractive about them. See if you can transfer these qualities to the seduction of your addiction.

2. You will probably find that the poem "turns" on you, as mine did when the wine bottle literally went looking for another victim.

3. Experiment with a repeating form (such as a pantoum) as the battle with alcohol involves doing the same thing over and over expecting different results.

4. Imagine that alcohol, or whatever compulsion fuels your addiction, is "out to get you." Imagine it tricks you somehow. Think of other activities you love and what attracts you about them. See if you can transfer these qualities to the seduction of your addiction.

In the following poem, I imagine a relapse. The prompt known as "meet me" can help you connect alcohol and alcoholism, (or any other addictive or compulsive behavior) with judgment and accountability. Adding some rhyme to make light of something that is not light will energize your writing. Try it.

Meet Me

Meet me between your thin pursed lips
and my fifth slip,

between the fantasy of just one more
and me in last night's dress, passed out on the floor

meet me between J&B and reverie; between the parking lot
and thanks a lot

Meet me between I'll always be your number one
and "What did you say your name was again, hon?"

Meet me between the bubbles and bumbles
the straight line and the stumbles

Meet me at the corner where faith and fear
part ways

Take my hand; help me get through
just one more day.

CONNECTION TO RECOVERY

I'm lucky not to have relapsed since 2006. Hearing relapse stories is critical to my avoiding complacency. The poem starts with a judgmental "other," who at the end turns into someone who can lend a hand. I need others to recover. And to remember it's one day at a time.

WRITING ABOUT YOUR FAMILY HISTORY

Your wounds probably began before you were born. We may have had parents, grandparents or even older ancestors who were alcoholics, addicts, or exhibited some other deep dysfunction. Exploring their wounds and disappointments helps us develop compassion for them and explain how we came to develop our own wounds. Trauma that occurred in our families before we were born can be transmitted to us.

We can begin this healing work by writing what we know about our parents and grandparents' lives and questioning what we don't know.

Don't worry about what you don't know about the past. Buried memories will return. When I began recovery, my parents were long dead. My sources of family information were few. When asked to make a list of major life events that had occurred before adolescence, I realized I had big gaps in my memory. This is common, as many children of alcoholic or dysfunctional families "froze" in traumatic moments. Our protection was denial. Nevertheless, this is the place to begin your writing work.

Ancestors

If you have done any genealogical research, you can write about ancestors you have discovered, even if you know very little about their lives. I researched ancestors on both my mother and father's sides. My mother had an ancestor named James Hardy (1820-1879) who emigrated from London to Philadelphia in 1841. My father's ancestor, Harald Haraldson (1824-1902) emigrated from Norway to Illinois is 1875. Although Haraldson came to this country much later than Hardy, these men were roughly the same age. That gave me the idea to invent a correspondence between them in their early thirties, as if they knew that their descendants—my mother and father—would meet and marry and that my father would become an alcoholic.

September 1, 1855,
From James Hardy, Philadelphia, Pennsylvania
to Harald Haraldson, Hjartdal, Norway

Dear Harald,

It's not the city of brotherly love.
Not yet. It's not a brand of cream cheese,
silver box with neat blue script,
I've never seen a bagel, never will.

And you are not my brother.
Not yet. But it will come, my offspring
will meet yours.

We don't know, do we Harald,
have no idea that our genes
will meet in one hundred years,
Dick and Sue will meet, and mate,
my blue eyes will join yours.

For now, I eat brown bread,
thank God for sun and rain,
an alternating pattern mysterious
but in the good years,
alfalfa feeds the beef.

Dear James,

I don't know anyone who has left
for The New World. Thus far,
no one has been struck by wanderlust.
We are a steady folk, James, no longing
to be anywhere but where God planted us.

But my wife has been overcome by spirits,
sees birds soar over the fjords,
attentive to the flips and swish of fish,
that moment before the dive,
she says she sees a sign.

She comes home crying,
about the fierce piercing of flesh,
wrested out of water to an atmosphere
inhospitable to gills, fearing it's a sign
to escape to different waters.

But I see it differently.
I feel the pain he will surely cause,
my great grandson Dick, not just to Sue
but to his children too, and I think
can I forestall it, can I thwart this union
by staying safe in Norway?

Dear Harald,

Salted klippfisk is as foreign to me
as tamales will be to Dick and Sue.
But Dick will love some things you do—
pickled pigs feet, sardines, oysters.

Your great grandson will also
take to peanuts, packed tightly
in a Mr. Peanut jar. Will he get his taste
for salt from you, or is it just a strategy
to balance out the booze?

CONNECTION TO RECOVRY

These poems assume a genetic tie to alcoholism, with ancestors who hope they can avoid the inevitable. Yet they are powerless. I became an alcoholic like my dad. ACA tells me that it was likely that I would both become alcoholic and be attracted to one as a mate. The poem also reminds us that alcoholism is a family disease, often going back for generations.

PROMPT:

1.Do some research on your ancestors and write a poem from the perspective of one or more of them, imagining what life will be like in the future.

2. Imagine that one of your addictions began in the past with one of these characters. Write about it.

3.If you don't know much about your ancestors, make up a story about what you imagine they were like or write about how you would like to find them.

In thinking about my family history, I saw the image of a ball of tangled yarn. My mother was accomplished in needlecraft, but she got tangled up with my father, a bitter alcoholic. And that made my childhood chaotic and crazy. I also like the fact that "yarn" means two things--a story and wool to knit with. Words with double entendres or ambiguity often attract me.

Here is a poem that takes a knitted scarf and pulls it apart, a metaphor for what we do with our family "story" when we examine what really happened.

The Scarf

I find it in the attic, a knitted jumble.
The moths have had their way, birthed
tiny winged creatures, left lacework in their wake.

I find an end, work loose a strand,
pull it gently, release the weave of years,
smooth out the long toughness of the yarn.

It falls in circles at my feet, like the first curls
of a daughter's hair, the curls her parents
could not bear to cut,

pasted in a baby book to mark a moment
when the beauty they had made
was enough to make them whole.

CONNECTION TO RECOVERY
The yarn connects the cyclical nature of alcoholism and the loss and sadness with something that once was beautiful, like a baby's curls. It reminds me that I was beautiful and perfect as a child. In recovery, I can become that way again.

PROMPT:

1. Think of your childhood and write about any object that seems significant to you.

2. Choose a specific object, like the yarn above, not an abstract idea.

3. What object do you have today that belonged to your mother, father or significant caretaker that seems to symbolize something about their lives?

4. Find an object from your parents or grandparents that seems odd or mysterious. Write about it and create its significance to your story.

5. Take your writing and put it into lines and stanzas. Experiment with different stanza lengths. Try one long stanza. See how this changes your work.

In the following poem, I take the same object—yarn—and make a List Poem by naming different types of yarn. Then I describe how each type of yarn relates to an aspect of living with an alcoholic. I repeat the initial consonant of the type of yarn and the abstract words, which adds "alliteration," the auditory appeal of repetition of an initial consonant.

You will notice in this next poem some proper names such as Sens Sens, Luckies, and Witnesses. I'm often asked if proper names "date" a poem or confuse the reader. The value of proper names is both specificity and auditory appeal. Sometimes, as with the word Luckies, you can also create a double meaning, as the cigarettes were not "lucky." If the emotional truth of the poem is clear to the reader without knowing the proper names, a poem is energized by specific details rather than abstract words. They may add to meaning if the reader looks them up but they will not detract if they are clear from the context.

Yarn

Mohair for mother, for the mystery
of a mistake, for marrying
too young, for miserable mornings.

Angora for anger, for accusations:
he's not good enough for you,
don't think that you can change him.

Chenille for cheap, for hand-me-downs,
the Outgrown Shop, children's clothes
threadbare in the knees.

Shetland for swearing off, for Sen Sens
squirreled into pockets; Shetland
for suffering the slings of hope.

34

Worsted, for it gets worse; no job,
waylaid into bars; wine-soaked
dart games, Luckies, out of luck.

CONNECTION TO RECOVERY

The list acts as a container for sadness, grief, and memory. The use of repeating sounds in each stanza reminds me of the repeating nature of family dysfunction.

PROMPT:

1.Look back at your free-writes where you wrote a list of some sort. Find an item on the list that resonates with you and then write a "list poem," of similar items, connecting them to a childhood memory.

2.Give the objects in your list a "voice" and allow them to tell you something important, perhaps even a mystery of your childhood. Don't worry about whether it is the truth or invented. If you can invent it, it has a seed of truth somewhere in your subconscious.

3.Some good items for lists are items from your childhood: games, foods, songs, books. You may surprise yourself by finding a common thread.

Parents' Marriage

I tried to imagine what must have been my mother's disappointment in her marriage to an alcoholic by writing about her wedding day. I have only a newspaper announcement of the wedding and a photo of my mother in a borrowed satin wedding dress. Was she so in love, at age 19, that she ignored the warning signs that my father was already an alcoholic? I took the image of a wilted bouquet to "hold" the disappointment that she may have sensed was coming. Then I converted the poem to a pantoum (I explain the form previously), which seemed appropriate, as it circles around central lines, and life with an alcoholic often feels like an endless repetition of anger, resignation and hope that this time it will be different.

Wedding Day

Mired in the muck of love, she said I do,
floating down the aisle in a veil of gossamer
thin as wisps of dandelion on the wind
Her satin gown a borrowed hand-me down

Floating down the aisle in a veil of gossamer
Could she foresee the flowering of weeds?
Her satin gown a borrowed hand-me down
a kiss, a ring, a vow, a change of heart

Could she foresee the flowering of weeds?
Her bouquet wilting from the start
a kiss, a ring, a vow, a change of heart
Entwined by vines that twisted vows to lies.

Her bouquet wilting from the start
Her satin gown a borrowed hand-me-down
entwined by vines that twisted vows to lies
Mired in the muck of love, she said I do.

This poem creates compassion for my mother, who married too young and doubtless with much hope that the dashing young Naval officer, Dick Beck, would get her off her parents' farm and into "real life." She didn't know that he was an alcoholic. She didn't know he would never become a journalist. She didn't know she would be stuck on the same farm—a gift from her parents—until she left my father when I was thirteen. Today I can see that she was attracted to him as I was attracted to dramatic men whose charm and energy overcame my fears. When I view my mother as guiltless in her choices, I feel compassion for her.

PROMPT:

1. Find an object, such as the wedding bouquet above, that can be a metaphor for feelings that you imagine your parents or caretakers owned before you were born. In my poem above, the wedding bouquet stands for the marriage itself. Look at old photographs to help you. Take that image and let it unfold. Keep writing until you surprise yourself.

2. Don't be afraid to completely change your poem once you have found the kernel of what you want to write about. I began Wedding Day, above, writing about my own wedding and my dress. But then I started wondering about my mother's wedding dress and the fact that she told me she borrowed it. I never saw it except in a photograph. Suddenly, I realized that I was more interested in her wedding than writing about mine.

Family Secrets

When I was about one year old, my grandfather fell in love with a much younger woman named Gladys, asked my grandmother to move from their farm in New Jersey to Reno, Nevada, for six weeks to establish residence so he could get a quick divorce. He apparently met Gladys at the Princeton Tavern, as town records for 1947 say she was an office manager there. Today, I wonder why my grandmother agreed. My grandmother was a gentle, caring person who always behaved as a lady. But to travel on her own to Reno must have been a frightening and bitter experience. She was forced to leave the farm where she had fed and housed farm hands for her entire adult life. My grandfather then moved Gladys into the "big house" on the farm. My grandmother moved into an apartment in Princeton, and worked nights as a telephone operator for Princeton Hospital. Today it occurs to me that my grandfather probably offered to support my grandmother. Perhaps her job was a passive-aggressive message that he had mistreated her. I knew these "facts," but until I considered the upheaval this must have caused my entire family, including my mother, twenty years old with a baby daughter and no doubt distraught over her father's betrayal of her mother, did I start to understand what emotional chaos must have surrounded my infancy. I have no memory of any of this, but I can answer how most people would have reacted.

By the time I was aware, Gladys was gone. Apparently the marriage lasted only a short time. My grandparents lived in separate houses until I was ten, but they attended family functions as if they were married. This poem shows that abandonment and its fallout had seeds before I was aware of family dysfunction.

Gladys

My grandma flew to Reno to give my grandpa
what he wanted: six weeks' residence, then

a divorce. Abandonment. Gladys, red-
haired harridan, upended thirty years'

of marriage when she stole my grandpa
at the tavern. Bitch is what my grandma

called her. That's what my mother said she said.
I never heard my grandma swear.

The marriage lasted for a year. Maybe
Gladys wouldn't go to Reno, give him

a divorce. She hovered in our family
like biting flies around a salt lick.

CONNECTION TO RECOVERY

Secrets "hovered" in our family. We adopted the
"don't feel; don't trust, don't talk" rule. No one dared
blame my grandfather. Today I can choose another way
to live. I can ask questions. I can connect mystery to
loss and grief. And I can recognize when authority
figures created fear or kept me from telling our truth.

My grandparents were divorced from 1947 until 1964, when they remarried. Why then? Family lore said Gladys would not agree to a divorce for almost twenty years. Today, that story strikes me as unlikely. My grandfather was back with my grandmother within two years of their divorce. My mother and I were the only ones who attended their remarriage when I was in High School, at which my grandmother wore a huge diamond ring, the only outward sign of my grandfather's guilt.

My grandfather bought a lovely farm in Hopewell, New Jersey called Ivy Rock, where he and my grandmother lived, unmarried, from 1958 to 1964. Throughout my High School years, I spent a lot of time at their farm, sleeping over on the weekends, watching the horses graze beyond my organdy curtains, awakened by the bleating of the sheep. During the night, the grandfather clock would sound on the hour. Like a puppy, comforted by a ticking clock when separated from its mother, I loved the regularity of that clock. In the poem below, I chose the clock to reveal my need for comfort. After my grandmother died, my family took turns choosing her possessions. I regret not choosing the clock, as the clock holds the sadness of what is gone, the connection between us. This poem holds complex emotions—mine and hers

Grandfather Clock

The clock was neat, compact, well mannered as my grandma,
a city girl transplanted to corn fields and a dairy farm.
Three feet of mahogany, centered on the mantel
of a fieldstone farmhouse called Ivy Rock.

In an ironed shirtwaist dress and tasteful pumps,
Mondays, she washed and ironed. Tuesdays,
with orange stick, clear polish, she manicured her nails.
Wednesdays, she played piano while I sang of ribbons, bonnets.

The clock kept life in check: the sheep released to bleat
at six am. Horses in at five. Lawrence Welk began his bubbles
right at eight on Saturdays.

When she died, we chose our favorite item first.
I don't know what I chose. But not the clock.
Some nights, I think I hear it. Others, I can almost see
the empty face that bound us, impassive in the dark.

CONNECTION TO RECOVERY

The clock symbolized the comfort and regularity of my grandparents' home, in stark contrast to my parents' house. I know now that just because no one raised his voice does not mean there was no tension or unhappiness in the house, but something about the life of a farm, the animals, their need for regular feeding, their movement into the pasture, made me feel safe. Even as a child, I had a great need for relief, the need that I ultimately satisfied with alcohol. It is good to remember that there are other ways to create relief and comfort.

PROMPT:

1.Choose an object, like the grandfather clock, that holds a memory for you about your childhood. Explore the object and tell a family story using the object as a focal point.

2."Implicate yourself in the poem." This means to make yourself responsible for the action. Perhaps you did not act in a totally truthful or commendable way. In the poem, I confess I didn't choose the clock, and the reader can imagine that I now regret that decision, particularly as I can't even recall what I did choose.

Today, I have two figurines on my dressing table that were my grandmother's. I don't recall how I got them, but I do recall treasuring them in childhood. These figurines helped me imagine my grandmother's early life. She was a city girl in Indianapolis. My grandfather grew up in the Indiana countryside, the son of a teacher. But after a short stint in college, he decided to take a herd of Jersey cows to New Jersey for a man who owned the farm my grandfather would manage and ultimately buy. My grandpa was not an alcoholic, but he was a dramatic personality.

Two Figures in Search of a Story

They used to live at grandma's house.
Now they live at mine. When she
died, they must have moved in here.
I must have wanted them.

Let's call her Maybelle. Let's call him John.
Maybelle is fair-skinned, full-skirted, tip-toed
in anticipation, she leans forward, eyes closed,
trusting in the promised kiss. John,
black-capped, clasps flowers at his back.

I must imagine it, almost all of it, where
they came from, what signified, why
they survived. They sit on my bookshelf,
china figurines atop square pedestals.

Even if I force
the pedestals to touch,
the lovers never will.

My city grandma, honeymooning with a farmer
from Kendalville at the Hotel Frontenac
in Quebec, may have spied them in the gift shop.
Were they a romantic trifle bought by her new husband?

Maybelle and John stayed together as a pair,
no stroke or tuberculosis, no pitchfork-
punctured lung, no four-pack days,
no Gladys from the feed mill,
no trip to Reno, no divorce.

CONNECTION TO RECOVERY

The more I write, the more I realize what I don't and will never know about my parents and grandparents. Exploring their hurts and decisions through the lens of recovery allows me to see that I idealized or demonized people from my past, when they were actually more nuanced. I humanize them. I forgive them. And I begin to forgive myself.

PROMPT:

1.Find an object in your home that came from your parents or grandparents. Imagine what story it would tell about them when it was in their home. Allow the object to reveal questions to you about what you don't know about your parents or grandparents. Write from the standpoint of wonder and compassion.

2.It's hard to imagine our parents or grandparents being young or perhaps foolish. Put them in some situation you have faced and see what happens.

A family with a secret often has more than one. Gladys was a secret I was not forced to keep, but my grandfather had a girlfriend named Francis later in his life that I kept secret from my grandmother. I met Francis in his hospital room after he had a tragic car accident in which he struck and killed a child. That brought on an attack of emphysema.

I was summoned home from college because the doctors thought he was dying. When I got to his room with my mother, there was Francis (my mother's age) sitting on the side of his bed. When he died a few years later, my mother gave me the job of calling Francis.

The Manicure

A young Korean man bends over me.
A shock of black hair hides his face.

He takes my hand in his.
I am embarrassed by the age
spots sprouting on my skin.
He clips my nails, oblivious.
To him, I'm just a client.

Then I recall my grandfather,
a lean, laconic farmer, gasping
through ravaged lungs in the hospital,
attended by the woman he had decided,
fearing death, he wanted me to meet.

Her name was Francis.
Francis from the feed mill.
She was my mother's age.

Here, seemingly in secret
from my grandmother,
Francis held his hands in hers
and gently clipped his nails

45

as if seated at the feet of Christ.

This gesture, more shocking
than a kiss or exposed flesh,
silenced small talk.
The silence grew, divisive,
deadly, deft.

CONNECTION TO RECOVERY

AA has a slogan: "You are as sick as your secrets." This is true of both the secrets about myself and the secrets I have kept for other people. I'm not sure how I justified keeping this secret for my grandfather, but I'm sure he knew neither I nor my mother would tell my grandmother. There was a cost in keeping this secret. I did not allow either of us to be our true selves.

PROMPT:

1. Write about any secret that you have kept for someone else, particularly if you were conflicted and wanted to tell the truth.

2. Write about any situation in which you learned a secret that changed the way you felt about someone you looked up to.

WRITING ABOUT YOUR CHILDHOOD LOSSES OR WOUNDS

My character trait of judgment and contempt is similar to my mother's reaction to her marriage. She must have been defiant when she insisted on marrying my father over her father's objection. Her addiction to drama and to secrets arose from the family "secret" of Gladys, the woman my grandfather fell in love with and for whom he abandoned my grandmother right before I was born. These traits were passed along to me.

These stories "explain" why I became the way I did. They also connect me to all other people in recovery, alcoholic or not, who were raised by dysfunctional or alcoholic parents.

Where to begin to explore these losses? I suggest you make a list of significant events that have taken place in your life. Begin at your birth. Events that occurred before you were conscious of them may be some of the most important. For example, I know I was born in Portsmouth Naval Hospital because my father was stationed there in the navy. I spent my first month in an incubator, as I was premature. Did I feel isolated, even as an infant? After my dad left the service, my parents drove to New Jersey with me on the back seat to what would become my home for the next thirteen years. What did they talk about on that trip? Where did they stop? Were they thrilled to have a baby girl or burdened by me?

Here is a partial list of the type of events to put on your list:

> *Birth of a Sibling*
> *Illness—your own or anyone in your family*
> *Weddings*
> *Starting School*
> *Divorce or breakup in your family or one close to you*
> *Friends move or become estranged*
> *Death of a family member or someone close to you*
> *Financial problem—someone loses a job, is demoted, etc.*

Moving
Change in Caregiver
Changing schools
Successes or defeats—sports, academics
Being bullied or being a bully
Jealousies of another

Remember that so-called "happy" events create stress too. Family vacations, family parties, weddings – all are important. Try to imagine how you felt during these events.

When we reclaim the pain, we strip it of its power. Don't worry if you can't remember. Feelings and buried memories will surface. In the meantime, imagine "how an ordinary child might have reacted." This freed me from trying to actually remember and allowed me to experience the grief or stress that must have been present when major events in my family occurred.

Before recovery, I knew I had buried memories. Haunted by a sense of dread, I tried to think my way into the past. My body's response— anxiety, a tightness in my throat, a clenching in my stomach—told me that something bad had happened. Then I realized that I was looking for one big traumatic event. Maybe there was no such event. I ultimately decided that I would discover what I needed to know when I needed to know it, relying on my Higher Power to reveal memories when I was able to handle them.

Writing about what I don't remember has helped me uncover the feelings underneath my fears. I become more patient.

I Don't Remember

Forget. Forget-me-nots.
Knots. Twisted shifting stems
of not enough. Where are they?

I don't remember.

Forgotten. Like the violets,
sprung up in the field, wild,
choked by growing leaves.

Where was he? Where was I?
Was there a moving van? Was he
standing on the stoop? Don't go!

Leaving. How did I get here?
Jump/cut. Frame 1: painting my
desk from brown to white.

Frame 2: pink ruffled bed skirt.
Organdy curtains. How did I
get here? I forgot.

Names of flowers, states on diner
placemats. State of dejection.
Despair? Euphoria?

The violets have died.
Next year, they'll pop up again
but I won't be there.

Next year, I'll be in the ruffled
bedroom. Where will you be?
I don't remember.

CONNECTION TO RECOVERY

Even if I can't recall situations, I know either how I felt or how an ordinary child would have felt. There is relief in allowing myself to be ordinary. There is also relief in knowing I don't have to search for one big traumatic event to be worthy of recovery. I can be patient and wait for memories to surface in my Higher Power's time.

PROMPT:

1. Write about any childhood event that you know was significant, but which you can't recall. It could be moving, first day at school, any event you suspect you have denied recalling.

2. Connect with a feeling of dread from your childhood. Does that dread connect with any person, place, or thing?

3. Notice that the poem above feels fractured, disjointed, as if the narrative is not clear. That is intentional. Don't try too hard to connect the dots. Just see what bubbles up.

Childhood Experience of Death

For many in recovery, our parents tried to shield us from death of someone close to us, believing that we were too young to "understand." They thought if they didn't talk about it, we would not feel the grief, wonder what was wrong, be confused about where the loved one went. Our parents were well-intentioned, but we absorbed the hurt and loss. Sometimes we thought we did something wrong. But we knew better than to talk about it. We learned confusion, denial of feelings, and not to talk.

I had a brother born when I was almost 4. He died shortly after birth due to a blood allergy. I have no memory of that event. I don't know where I stayed when my mother was in the hospital. The baby never came home from the hospital. Yet, recently, looking through some old photographs, I came across a tiny birth announcement my mother had sent to my aunt. It's in my mother's handwriting. It's dated November 25, 1951. My brother was three days old.

The following day he died of the Rh negative blood disorder. I found a telegram from my father to his parents informing them of the death. So much hope was embodied in that tiny birth announcement. The telegram, by contrast, is stark. "Baby boy developed toxic condition due RH factor. Lived only four days. Services were today. Ashes will be dedicated to memorial tree at our home. We are all well and resigned. Love. Dick" The word "resigned" seems so poignant. How did I, almost four, absorb what must have been a time of terrible disappointment and grief? I have no memory. What tree is Danny buried under? No one ever told me there was a burial tree on our farm.

Baby boy.

Lived only four days.
Services today.
We are all well and
Resigned.
Lived only four days.
Toxic condition.
Blue ribbon on the card.
His name was Daniel.
Daniel. Baby boy.
Resigned.
Love, Dick.
Baby boy.

CONNECTION TO RECOVERY

The grief of my brother's death must have affected my parents in ways that were transmitted to my other brother, Peter, and me. Even if I can't recall it, that wound lives within me. Grieving is a process that used to baffle me. I thought there was some secret ritual or ceremony called "grieving." A wise woman told me, "you just talk about it until you don't have to talk about it anymore." Of course, that usually requires a listener, a witness to our grief. I have to overcome the fear that I am bothering the listener, or that I should "be over it" by now. This is one of the gifts we offer each other in recovery: listening with love and without trying to fix things, change things, or make them go away.

PROMPT:

1. Take a family memory and "translate it" into a telegraph format. Knowing that every word in a telegraph costs money, think carefully about what words to repeat. The repeating words gain weight. Start and end with the same line.

2. Notice I added the baby's name, which was not in the original telegram. What would you add? What seems important to add, even if you don't know the answer?

53

I recall years later my mother telling me that she and my father were told not to have any more children, as they would have the same blood disorder. Yet in 1955, my brother Stephen was born. He was transfused twice at birth to get him clean blood. What a risk my parents took! Was my mother scared to death throughout her pregnancy, as I would have been? If so, I have no memory of it. But I know that as a seven-year-old, that anxiety and tension must have permeated my unconscious.

Children weren't told much about death when I was young. Adults kept their grief a secret. But those secrets affected us then and they affect us today. The fact that the baby was named Daniel shows that to my parents, he was a child. My brother named his first son Daniel. Baby Daniel's death affected us all.

The Shame of Having an Alcoholic or Dysfunctional Parent

Our dairy farm in New Jersey was hidden from the main road by a quarter-mile rutted lane. My playmates were my three cousins, who lived on an adjoining farm. Both properties were owned by my grandfather, who set my uncle and father up as partners in the dairy farming business.

Within a year, my grandfather called off the partnership because my father proved unreliable. He'd show up for milking at 7am with a six-pack. This must have been a major disappointment to my mother. It must have created incredible financial anxiety. All I know is my father ended up as a milk truck driver for Sealtest Dairy. He was a graduate of Brown University. His separation papers from the navy list his profession as "journalist."

How do hopes and dreams move from "journalist" to "milk truck driver?" Alcohol, no doubt, was part of the explanation. In this poem, I tried to imagine what my father must have felt, knowing his family was disgusted with him and that my mother was teaching her children the only tool she had to cope: contempt.

Future Entrepreneurs of America

She's at it again – saving me from myself.
The army she's enlisted are my kids.
She's offered them a prize to prove a point.

A nickel for each bottle they can ferret out
and bring her, the best ones half full—
so she can have the fun of pouring
spirits down the kitchen drain.

They choose to think this doesn't hurt,
that I'm beyond humiliation – or else
I'd surely stop.

I hope they never get to be
a nickel's toss from hell.

CONNECTION TO RECOVERY

By writing in my father's voice, I allow him to voice his fears, which creates empathy. In the poem, he is aware that he can't stop drinking. This reminds me that his alcoholism was not a moral failing, as we believed at the time. It reminds me that alcoholism is a disease.

PROMPT:

1.Choose any painful memory from childhood and write about it from the point of view of another person in the story. If it's a parent, you may choose to write both their stories.

2.Experiment with dialogue. Turn your story into a poem where the two spouses each give their point of view.

3.Imagine that person had an emotional "bottom." Write about the bottom with the compassion you would extend if that were your bottom.

I never had friends come to my house. My father was too unpredictable. I was humiliated by his melodramatic and nasty ranting. Below, I wrote an invitation to Sunday dinner.

Sunday Dinner

Please come to Sunday dinner.
After, we'll play Scrabble with my brothers
who cheat and chortle, make up words.

Please ignore my drunken father
the egg he's cracked on mother's head,
the slow drip of yolk from her forehead
down her face, the stain she can't erase.

Ignore his scream from the kitchen,
his limp into the dining room, his
foot sliced open, blood oozing,

his cockeyed grin – the joke he
thinks we'll all enjoy: "Relax, kids,
it's only ketchup!

CONNECTION TO RECOVERY

I was powerless as a child, a witness to my father's brutal treatment of my mother, which I had to watch, like the yoke dripping down her face. His manipulation of his children's sympathy in a supposed "injury," which was actually a ketchup joke, was juvenile and cruel. Yet if we protested, he'd fly into a rage. Scenes like this show why I developed a need to hide, to pretend, and to walk on eggshells around my father.

PROMPT:

1.Write about a dinner table. Populate it with anyone you wish, actual people or imagined ones. Let them talk and see what they might say.

2.Start with a sincere invitation to something that sounds like fun. Then turn the scene to one that no one would want to attend.

3.Write about what you feared would happen if you had friends over as a child – or pick an actual time and bring your older self to reflect on what your younger self must have felt.

Violence and Feeling Unsafe

We who grew up in an alcoholic or dysfunctional family knew we were not safe. I wrote about walking home from school, fearing that I would find my father drunk and rageful. He rarely hit us, but he swore, red-faced with anger and contempt. His anger was inexplicable. What had set him off? Would he be funny and want to play softball or would he be passed out on the living room rug? That uncertainty was worse than predictability. It created chaos, a roller coaster ride of emotions.

In this poem what is in a newspaper—words—can be more damaging to a child than being hit. His words imprinted a belief that we were worthless and a problem. We were shamed and felt abandoned emotionally. This is true even if we witnessed these words being directed as others. When I first came into recovery, I said my dad picked on everyone except me. Today, I believe that was not true, but even if it were, I now know that if I was in the room, I didn't need to be the one being derided and cursed at to register the blow.

Walking Home

It's four o'clock. The school bus chugs off,
leaving me at the end of the lane to our farm.
It's called Princessville Road.

It's lined with dirt, brambles, scent of wild things:
ink berries, bittersweet – their poison packed
in blood-red berries bursting from their jackets,

cornflowers, huckleberries, honeysuckle,
tiny drops of nectar shimmering on the stem.
Pull them through a slender shaft and suck it dry.

My mother isn't home.
She's gone to work, and left me
to return to an empty house.

At least, I hope it's empty. I hope my father
won't be there, his rage rolled up like newspaper,
a weapon that's supposed to leave no mark.

CONNECTION TO RECOVERY

I see how I developed an addiction to the chaos of an alcoholic household. I also acknowledge that the newspaper—words—were also used as a weapon against me. Finally, I see that the natural world, even when it presented danger, is a "safe space" for me.

PROMPT:

1. Write about where you were when you realized you weren't safe.

2. Try to find an image, such as the newspaper in the poem above, to stand as a symbol for a weapon.

3. Try to put "contrary" impulses in your poem. They create energy. Notice that the seemingly peaceful scene of walking down the lane with the berries and flowers becomes for the narrator a scene of danger when she imagines that the berries are "poison." So the berries are simultaneously attractive and dangerous. This is one way to reveal what keeps us returning to dangerous or unsafe emotional or physical places. We make choices that recreate our past, even if the past was painful.

Abandonment, Physical or Emotional

Abandonment is a central wound of childhood that creates a great need for relief as we age, a need that we satisfy with a substance that relieves fear and feeling not good enough. We need not be left at an orphanage to feel abandoned. Parents who say or imply that we weren't wanted, that we were in the way, that our voices didn't matter, created a fear of abandonment. Abandonment is a form of violence.

My father was unreliable. He taught me not to trust. My mother would send me into bars to get him, a humiliating errand as well as pointless. I can recall the musty smell of bars, the darts and the dartboard, and sitting on the stool next to my dad being offered peanuts. Today, I know that my mother sending me there was wrong. I imagine her waiting outside as I sat in a dark bar in the middle of a sunny afternoon.

One day, my dad forgot to pick me up at the movies. In the following poem, I imagine the bar is like heaven for my dad. This image surprised me, but it shows some compassion for my father and his great need for relief. It wasn't until I began a program of recovery that I started to temper my anger with understanding.

Stood Up

I stood outside the Princeton Theatre,
awareness dawning slowly, as the sun began to set.

My father had forgotten me. It was clear as my face
reflected in the windows of Landau's Fine Woolens,

How could I compete with shots and beer at Sensi's Bar & Grill?
The wooden bar, worn to the comfort of an old shoe,

smoke rings from his Lucky Strikes wafting upward with soft
abandon, like a dancer's hula skirt, the foam slipping

over the pure clear glass, pooling in bright golden puddles,
heaven just within his grasp.

My dad was sick. He didn't deliberately forget me, which was how I felt then. He was seeking relief. I now know what that compulsion feels like. Today, I can recognize if someone is late or forgets an appointment with me, that I haven't been abandoned. I can set boundaries with friends who continually stand me up, but I can remind my Inner Child that I am an adult, able to set boundaries and make healthy choices.

PROMPT:

1.Write about someone who has abandoned you in the past.

2.Who triggers feelings of abandonment in you today?

3.Write about an incident when you felt abandoned or left to act in a role of responsibility that you didn't know how to handle.

4.Add a "simile" into your poem. A simile is a comparison of one thing for something that is not like it using "like" or "as." It serves the function of startling the reader with an unexpected opening up of the scene. When I say "clear as my face reflected in the windows of Landau's Fine Woolens," I am creating an image, a picture of a girl's face looking into a window of a store where there is something "Fine." But she is not fine. The image of smoke looking like a hula skirt compares the seedy bar to the paradise of Hawaii, a sad and sarcastic comparison. To the narrator, nothing about the scene is paradise. You can read more about similes in the Appendix.

By articulating what I wanted from my parents when I was young, I can see the feelings of loneliness and fear that underlie emotional abandonment. Here is a poem where the child calls on the parents for what the child needs:

Can Anybody Hear Me?

Father, I am calling.
Father, I am hungry.
Give me peanuts, clustered
tight in papery shells,
or oysters, wrested
with your knife from their
tight-lipped home,
how they hold themselves
together, resist opening.
They are quivering
helpless to resist.

Mother, I am calling.
Mother, I am hungry.
Give me oatmeal,
chocolate pudding.
Show me where to look
beneath the bushes for berries,
the artichokes unfolding
soft and sweet,
their center
worth the wait.

PROMPT:

1.Write a poem in which you ask your parents for food. Imagine foods that you associate with each of them, foods that perhaps you loved or had mixed feelings about.

2.Try to include in your request for food the idea that they were not listening to you and did not hear you.

The childhood game of Musical Chairs is the perfect example of a game designed to make a child feel left out. I hated it then and I still hate it. Being "left out" was a childhood fear that resulted from feeling not good enough and being different. That feeling has continued into adulthood. Games we played as a child often contain kernels of who we would become. As many of my friends in recovery know, I still show up at the diner to meet a large group of friends for breakfast convinced that all the seats will be taken and there will be no place for me. If nothing else, this has made me hyper-vigilant to see that no one else gets left out.

Musical Chairs

When I was five, when I had
one pink party dress, one pair
of white socks with eyelet trim,
when life seemed filled with not enough,

A party game that seemed designed
by monsters or an evil witch.
Peppy music played, I skipped around
a row of chairs, anticipating cake and goody bags.

As soon as I was lulled into my role
in this fairy tale, as soon as I heard
Disneyworld, or beach vacation, or
Good Job, Sweetie. You're the best--

The music stopped. Stunned.
Pause. And in that pause, the other
clever children, grabbed a chair,
nudged me over, sat down quick.

I stood. They stared.
Some kindly grownup took my
hand and leaned me up against the wall.
Where I'm still standing, in the land
of not enough to go around.

CONNECTION TO RECOVERY

The poem shows me that I'm still living in the land of "not enough to go around," a common feeling among alcoholics. I can practice being emotionally available today. I can practice being that adult who takes the child and leads me to a safe space.

PROMPT:

1. Write about any childhood experience in which you felt left out of an experience or game.

2. Find a game that can serve as a metaphor for your feeling of not being good enough.

3. Notice that I plant in the poem some lines of dialogue imagined by the narrator. In her fantasy, she heard praise, but in reality she was left without a chair. Think of words of praise you wanted to hear as a child and plant them in your poem.

4. Notice also that an adult shows up at the end and leans the narrator up against a wall. This was also unexpected, but this line links the narrator as a child with the narrator as an adult. She is no longer playing musical chairs, but she is standing alone and isolated, believing there is "not enough to go around." This last line is a play on words that echoes the game of musical chairs "going around." It is also literally a line about the child believing there is not enough of something, perhaps praise, or love, or talent, to make her feel good enough.

Feeling Not Good Enough

My primary feelings as a child were fear, loneliness, and shame. I learned this in the ACA program. When I began recovery, I identified fear—that seems a natural reaction to living with an angry alcoholic. But I didn't know I felt lonely, which is another word for abandoned. I didn't know I felt shame. That feeling can sneak up on me today. I need to recognize it, and help my Inner Child understand that she has a healthy, capable adult (me) taking care of her today.

Shame on You

When I had no words for feelings,
except happy, mad, or sad

When feelings were best conscribed
to children's books, Peter Rabbit

happy when he swiped the carrot,
mad when Farmer McGregor caught

him out, sad for the Pokey Little Puppy
who went to bed with no dessert

because he'd dug a hole, escaped
into the wide, wide world,

When feelings rhymed and showed up
at the end of lines,

I didn't know the sound at night,
repeated like a vacuum cleaner

was the blood careening in my temples
taking stock of all the slights, mistakes,

deprivations of the day. I knew
the comfort of my thumb in my mouth,

when, at ten, I was too big a girl
to suck my thumb,

twirling a strand of hair, hiding, hiding
but unable to resist, desist.

I knew I should be ashamed
of myself, I knew I shouldn't do it,
but it made me happy, or if

not happy, then numb, or maybe
even sad, with a sprinkling of angry,
maybe even that.

CONNECTION TO RECOVERY

Today I know that a ten-year-old who still sucks her thumb needs help. Shaming her is the last thing that will help. I can hold my Inner Child gently and reassure her that I will love and value her today.

PROMPT:

1.Write about anything you did as a child that you were criticized for as shameful.

2.Write about what was said to you that you felt shamed you.

My primary shame growing up was both my father's alcoholism and not having enough money. I don't recall ever going hungry, but I know there were things I wanted that we could not afford. There was nothing romantic about our farm. I was ashamed of our house. Built in 1741, today it has been restored to a historic landmark. But when I was growing up, the front door led to a pile of stones my father said he was going to make into a porch. Those stones stood for years as a symbol of his failures. I wanted a little house on a street with sidewalks. We had a well that ran dry in the summer. We hauled water in milk cans and took baths in the same dirty water. We had a quarter-mile brambled lane that scratched the paint of the sides of cars that ventured down. We would get snowed in for weeks, as it was not a public road. I tried to act like I lived on a gentleman's farm, but I doubt anyone believed me.

I was terrible at sports. I lived an isolated life on a hard-scrabble farm. I had few friends. But I loved school. Even now, I feel unsettled in June because the structure of the school year is ending. Back then, school was the safe place to be, the place where I knew what to do and could do it. But one day in second grade, I was accused of theft. I hadn't done it, but the fact that a teacher thought I stole money planted the seed that she thought I was a poor kid.

Privilege

*Clean the chalkboard for the teacher, press chalkdust
in small circles, erase "Dick, Spot, Sally," or the answer
to small sums, 2 + 2, projects simple and straightforward.*

*I longed to be the one to smack together the erasers,
release clouds of chalkdust in the air, to sift into my hair,
jumper, gritty signs of my anointing.*

*Who got picked? The one who answered right, could sound
out words, the line leader, the kind of girl whose mother
met her at the bus stop with a cookie and a hug.*

Not the kind of kid who tied her shoelace to the piano leg
at naptime, a knot that tightened with each panicked tug.

Not the kind of girl who claimed she was left-handed
when the teacher said to be left-handed was so rare
that few could claim the gift.

Not the one accused of stealing milk money from the cloakroom,
pilfered from the pockets of a second grader's coat,
a charge so stunning it trailed clouds of doubt.

CONNECTION TO RECOVERY

I've heard it said that men drink over resentments; women drink over shame. I'm sure this is over-simplistic, but it was true for me. My primary feeling that I tried to take away with drinking was shame.

PROMPT:

1.Think of a time when you were unfairly accused. Explore this event and how you felt.

2.See if you can find an image, like the chalk-dust in the poem above, that can hover over the poem like an accusation.

Another source of shame for me was not having the right clothes or enough of the right clothes. We had an expression in my family that I always thought was a "family word," *cattywampus*, meaning your buttons were not in the matching buttonhole. I was delighted when I found the word in a book about poetry written by the poet Ted Kooser. He used it as a metaphor for how to approach a poem, which

Emily Dickinson recommended to do "at a slant." Others have said to come in "the side door." When we sneak up on a poem without coming at it with a clear idea of opening the front door and striding in a straight line to the living room, we open ourselves to surprise and revelation. I used the word "cattywampus" to show that I felt perpetually not as "buttoned up" as my peers.

Cattywampus

> *colloquial, org: American Midwest:*
> *lopsided, crooked, misaligned*

I didn't trust myself to plaids or polka dots,
left all fashion risk to girls who could afford
to set the trends, like Papagallo flats, flowered
blouses from Liberty of London.

Each day, I'd dress in a round-collared shirt,
add a pleated skirt and cardigan, soft yellow,
peach, sometimes red or black, buttoned up.
A uniform demanding as a catechism.

My buttons seemed as neat as theirs. But danger lurked
in buttonholes. One Thursday, I showed up
buttoned cattywampus, sweater hem drooping
on the right, neckline off-balance on the left.

I walked the halls oblivious, slung school books
on my hip, betrayed by buttons, unaware
a part of me was permanently misaligned.

Oh, if only the "right" clothes could form the perfect mask. If I discard my disguises, I might reveal my True Self. Self- sufficiency is one of my favorite masks. As I grow in program, I wait for others to solve problems in meetings or volunteer. I pause before saying "yes" to commitments.

PROMPT:

1.Write about a favorite article of clothing from your childhood. See where it takes you.

2.Write about a word used in your family, a nickname, some kind of fun family word. If you don't have one, make one up.

3.Think of an image of something that made you feel different from your peers. It could be clothing, a hairstyle, your family car, anything that made you feel "less than." Explore the image.

My family used teasing and sarcasm as a passive-aggressive form of violence. Sometimes it was lighthearted. My nickname was "Tino." It came from a diminutive of Christine. My grandfather named his winning racehorse, Tino-Bets, which made me proud. But when I discovered a boy at summer camp with the name Tino on his towel, I felt betrayed. Hadn't my parents known they had given me a boy's name?

I also heard words and phrases, whether directed at me or in my presence, that were cruel and vengeful. "Don't flatter yourself," "You're no prize," "mama's boy," "cry-baby" and much worse. For some unknown reason, my father called us "pricks." I discovered a couple of these phrases bubble up into a poem I wrote about Ahab, the whaling ship captain on the hunt to kill Moby Dick. I wondered what type of trauma (I was assuming a leg lost to a whale's teeth was insufficient) would cause a man to put himself and his crew in mortal danger. My poem revealed that Ahab had been told he was worthless as a child. (I made this up.) The phrase "who do you think you are?" snuck into the poem. This poem is in Ahab's voice.

Ahab

I was out for blood. I don't deny it.
It was the constant pressure of the loss,

nerves that jangled in the dark,
a phantom of my familiar.

I stalked him, retribution hulking in the briny night.
The sea was black, flat, wanting only, what?

I heard a siren call, familiar as a nursery rhyme:
Who do you think you are? You're no prize. Mama's boy.

I formed the words: I'll show you who's in charge.
Then flung them in the wind. They sunk, feathers in a foaming sea.

White as New England snow, a blank page wanting explanation.
And then his eyes, a certainty that never looked straight on,

always sideways, shifty eyes reminding me
of someone, but who? Maybe you.

He blundered into me, rammed his forehead
against my story, my narrative of how it all began,

how it should end, cut in half my final chapter.
He wound me up and reeled me in.

Sucked into his vortex, he had me after all.

PROMPT:

1. Write about names you remember being called as a child. See if you can "plant" them in a poem that is not directly about you.

2. Write a poem in which you overhear a child being called a name you were called. Imagine you confront the parent. What would you say? How could you come at this "slant?" Captain Ahab is about as different from me as a character could be, yet I found something compelling in his energy that I could relate to.

Hypervigilance

I learned to deal with the fear of violence by being hypervigilant to the moods in my house. I learned to hide. I wrote about it, using the game "Huckle, Buckle Beanstalk," a game of searching for an object in plain view. The name had that wonderful sound of repetition that I treasure in writing poetry. I thought the game was harmless fun, but uncovered a deeper meaning. See if you can keep writing about a topic until you surprise yourself with a kernel of a buried truth.

I surprised myself by turning into a tree. This is called a "turn" in poetry, a shift in tone or topic. Growing up, I always felt safe outside sitting under a tree, so it isn't surprising that I turned myself into a tree. I made the tree a home that has "sustenance," plenty of what is needed to nurture birds and bugs—and maybe me.

Objects

Huckle buckle beanstalk, a game of looking
for an object hidden in plain view, which
refuses to be found, camouflaged
in the shift and twist of the material.

An ordinary object, a pencil, say, or glove,
something useful, or something useless,
a ticket stub from a movie, a dried rose
from a man whose name has frittered off.

I loved that game, where luck was immaterial,
where skill or speed, or being chosen for the team,
was unimportant, a game for which you needn't trust
another, no secret word, no acting out a movie title.

Just silent vigilance, looking for what isn't there, or
isn't where it's supposed to be, knowing you are what
is missing, which is why you love to hide in open air,
stashed in plain view, looking ordinary. Slowing down

your breathing, until you sink into a nearby sapling, not worth
noticing. Until you are the tree, a home for birds and bugs,
a stationary object that sucks up sustenance
from deep inside the earth.

PROMPT:

1.Write about your backyard, park, or wherever you played outside as a child. Who was there? What games did you play? Did you feel safe?

2.Write about your relationship with nature and the natural world today. Is it a safe, inspiring place? Try to imagine a safe place and write about it. Allow birds or animals to talk or help you if they want to.

Sexual Abuse and Sexual Confusion

Some of us were sexually abused as children. Far more of us have a vague feeling that something was done to us but have no clear memory. This feeling undercuts our recovery and leads to a constant, nagging wondering about the "truth." At its most horrific, childhood sexual abuse involves rape. But when we consider sexual abuse as any un-consented contact of a sexual nature, which can extend to comments on our sexuality or body, we find we frequently recall experiences that affected us with a deep sense of shame and violation. That shame frequently led to the need for relief that alcohol or other addictions provide.

The "#Me-Too" movement widened our understanding of sexual assault from date-rape, to actions such as groping or kissing women without their consent or invitation. Many of us recall conduct or comments that made us feel unsafe in our bodies. Our sense of innocence was betrayed. Our ability to trust was fractured. I wrote this poem called "Safe House" thinking about these issues:

Safe House

You can't touch me here.
You can't knock on my door,
scratch at my windowpane.

You can't call me baby,
whisper my name,
You can't act like you're in charge.

Did I ask you to? Did I?
What did I do? Is nothing,
something?

What something, then, did I do?
Give you directions?
Or maybe just make eye contact?

What was I supposed to do?
Look down. Shut up.
How many excuses for you
do I have to conjure up?

CONNECTION TO RECOVERY

I needed to separate out shameful acts initiated by others from the idea I invited them. As a child, I can recall only one incident where I "told," when my first boyfriend's father grabbed me on their couch and tried to kiss me. I told my mother and she told his mother. I have no memory of what happened next. I'm pretty sure I never got an apology.

As you explore your earliest memories of sexuality, write about your first kiss, first sex, etc. The following is a poem that shows both denial and an effort to get at the truth.

First Kiss

Here's the one I talk about.
At fourteen, my teenage boyfriend
off to summer camp
a kiss goodbye in his garage
that set my head awhirl,
like Rhett and Scarlet on steroids.

But he was not the first.
My first kiss was Billy Teague,
a neighbor boy.
Billy rode my school bus
grabbed me one day
in the backseat.

He put his tongue in my mouth.
It was not fun, romantic, sweet.
It felt mean. I thought he hated me.

Another kiss
another tongue
This time visiting my dad in rehab.

I was thirteen.
He met us for a family visit
in the parking lot,
acted like Jack Nicholson
in Cuckoos Nest.
Rehab wasn't working,
whatever it was supposed to do.

If he wasn't drinking, this was worse
than drinking. Manic. Barking like a dog.
Then my father leaned into the backseat
and pushed his tongue into my mouth.
Was he daring me to tell?
Or did he know, even then,
the power he could wield
like a knife stuck in my guts?

CONNECTION TO RECOVERY

Telling my secrets, even if they don't seem that bad or dramatic, helps me recover feelings. The memory of visiting my dad in rehab today strikes me as unlikely. Why would he be released to visit his family in a parking lot? Am I recalling a dream? All I know is that the memory is deep and strong. I need to trust it as part of my truth.

PROMPT:

1.Reflect in quiet about your earliest awareness of sexuality. Where were you? What happened? What conclusions did you come to about your feelings and those of others? Write about your experiences.

2.Think of any time someone touched you in a sexual way that was unwelcome to you. How did you respond? Did you keep the incident a "secret?" How has secrecy affected your sex life in later years?

Another early memory of a sexual assault occurred in Junior High School. A group of boys decided to walk up to girls who were developing breasts and swat their breasts. We'd drop our books. They'd laugh. This was actually painful. And as they often came up from behind me, it was frightening. I don't think I was the only girl affected but I can't recall any other girl talking about this behavior. I certainly didn't tell the school. I guess I wanted to pretend it wasn't happening or that I was cool. It now makes me very angry.

Batting Practice

Holding books tight to my chest,
boys in the hallway of my Junior High
would knock the books out of my hands,
bat me in the breasts,
guffaw, run, high five.
Like I was a basketball
being dribbled
passed to the guy on the left.
Slam dunk
Slam
It wasn't so bad
No bruises
Not bad enough to complain
Lucky
Was I lucky?

CONNECTION TO RECOVERY

I often default to "it wasn't so bad" in thinking about my childhood wounds. But it was bad enough. I don't need to compare myself to others. I don't need to earn my seat at the recovery table. Trying to be "cool" was always a trap for me.

Break-up of the Family of Origin

My mother didn't leave my father until I was fourteen. By then, her job could support us. By that time, we had nothing to mourn about leaving the farm. But it had been home for fourteen years and was imbued with a strong sense of history. As we painted furniture in our old house to take to our new one, I knew we were moving. But, like many Adult Children I have big gaps in my memory. How did we move our furniture? Where was my father when we left? What did he say about our moving out? Logic tells me it was a huge melodramatic scene, but in my memory, one day we lived on the farm and the next day we lived in town. I don't recall approaching the move with hope or even relief, although I imagine those feelings must have been there. But it was change, big change, and I'm sure the dread of change inspired feelings like the dead moth that appears at the end of this poem (an example of the surprise that can happen).

Starting Over

When my mother kicked my father out,
silence tumbled in.

Our farmhouse had been furnished
in old wood, mahogany and oak--

the dining table, desk, and bookshelves,
even bedsteads, all evoked the color

of brown dirt, dark and dank, as when
the plow clears last year's stalks away.

We painted it all white. For weeks,
we made each piece as pure as baby's breath.

With each stroke, I covered fourteen years.
They lay stuck in drying paint, like a moth,

when it surrenders to the trap, its wings
turned hard and gray.

Like the moth, I was trapped as a child in an alcoholic home. That feeling of being trapped can be triggered in adulthood. A better alternative to a drink is to speak to my Inner Child and remind her she is not trapped today.

PROMPT:

1. Think about a piece of furniture, flooring or wallpaper from your childhood home. Let it speak for you about the loss of your home, even if you didn't think it was a loss.

2. Write about any move you made in childhood, trying to capture the mixed emotions any move entails.

Today my childhood home has been bought by the town of Lawrenceville, New Jersey and turned into a museum called the Brearley House. As a child, I never considered that other people had lived there from 1761 until 1948. Ironically, that the house is now "restored" as a historic museum as if it never contained hurt or pain, angry words or frightened children. When I went back to see it, a ten inch square of my bedroom wallpaper has been preserved under plexiglass to show what the house looked like before they restored it. My feelings are trapped under glass, like a butterfly in a collection.

The Brearley House

There's a gift shop where my kitchen used to be.
Neat stacks of aprons, sweatshirts, baseball caps
exclaim: "The Brearley House, 1761." Here, my bedroom
stripped of wallpaper my mother chose –
square dancers, arms linked in cheery circles.

Growing up, this farm was ours, as if we'd always been its boss.
But there were others here before us.

They cooked over my fireplace, knew which wide-planked
floorboards creaked, trod the secret path to the apple trees,
dried black walnuts in the attic, wrested blackberries
from entangled leaves.

Perhaps they had a daughter who hung laundry on the line,
sheets snapping at her face. I wonder if they're buried here,
like my dad, his ashes under our first Christmas tree,
now tall with certainty, as if it can't recall when I was five,
and it was only two feet high, twinkling with lights and mystery.

CONNECTION TO RECOVERY

"Home" is a trigger for alcoholics and Adult Children.
The fact that mine has been memorialized as a museum,
neatened up and shining, underscores the mask that I
tried to wear as a kid, telling friends I lived on a "farm,"
as if it were romantic, with race horses galloping in the
pasture, cows grazing, and bunnies with red eyes
squirming in their cages. I remember that I wore a mask
to disguise hurt and feeling different. Today I can be my
True Self.

Losing Friends

My aunt, uncle and cousins moved from the farm across from ours in New Jersey to Maryland, in 1958. I don't remember the day they left, but I realized in making my timeline that this was a major event. My three cousins were my only playmates, as we were isolated on the farm. My father's violent behavior meant we didn't invite people to visit. Suddenly, my girl cousins were gone, leaving me with two younger brothers. When was I told they were leaving? How did I feel? Was I lonely or scared? I have no recollection. I was ten.   I found a photograph of me and my cousins from an Easter when I was six and used the image of little children with their hands held open as if to receive some treasure as a metaphor for the emptiness that was coming.

> Easter at the Cemetery
>
> We are posed leaning on gravestones
> in the small graveyard next to the
> white clapboard Presbyterian Church
> where my parents married. I'm wearing
> white organza and a ruffled collar.
>
> Our hands are cupped together,
> four cousins, two girls, two boys,
> as if we wait for something magical.
> Petals? Pennies? Jelly beans?

What did we think was our reward for staying
crisp and starched, smiling for the camera?

I can't imagine now. Can't fathom what we could
have thought was coming next. Whatever
bounty we expected, our hands are empty.

CONNECTION TO RECOVERY

The feeling of abandonment, of being left behind, still haunts me. I remind my Inner Child that feelings like this can be healed, and she was not at fault. Even if I don't recall what was said when my cousins left, I can write to them today and tell them. I don't need to mail the letter.

PROMPT:

1.Think of a time when you lost a friend or playmate, either because he or she moved, you moved, or some other life event took place. See if you can find a photograph of you to write about. Or think of a place you liked to play or a game you played.

2.Write about a family holiday, where you felt that things were not the way they should be. Use any of these images to write about the experience of playing with your friend.

3.If you remember how or why your friendship changed, envision the scene in which it occurred. If there was no scene, make one up. Imagine what you would have said or what your friend would have said. Add dialogue to express what you failed to communicate.

4.Plant a metaphor in your poem. In this poem, the metaphor of the cupped hands is that heaven is going to put some kind of bounty into the children's hands. The bounty is an illusion, but the children don't know it.

My mother converted to a Jehovah's Witness when I was ten. We kids became Witnesses too. Being a Jehovah's Witness fed my growing judgmental characteristics, a survival skill to combat my sense of not being as good as everybody else. Jehovah's Witnesses believed they were saved and the rest the world were going to burn up in the war of Armageddon. One part of me thought this was crazy and wrong. Another part liked being special. We were required to log in the hours we spent in "field service," going door-to-door with the Watchtower and Awake magazines.

I lost a girlfriend in adolescence. As a result of what I said, my friend JoAnn's mother decided we wouldn't see each other anymore. We were cut off by her family. I didn't see her mother again until sixteen years later at my mother's funeral. I never saw JoAnn again. But I know her mother complained to my mother about me. If my mother consoled me or talked to me about what happened or asked about my feelings, I don't recall.

Zest

Casting our bodies into the ocean
posing in the roles of a TV commercial,
we'd dive under a foaming wave,
then emerge, arms held high in a V,
laughing, shouting "Zest!"

JoAnn had dark curly hair,
perpetually pinned up
in orange juice cans. Mine
was straight as raw spaghetti.

We were fourteen, floating in the bubble
before boys were all we'd talk about.
Sleepovers in her tiny apartment,
her mom's Italian broccoli soup,
enticing as an enchilada.

One Saturday morning, in her living room,
gathering to go "in service" door-to-door
with the Watchtower, JoAnn's mom and aunt
seemed to dawdle over gossip and coffee.

Whatever I said, it must have sounded like,
 "You'll never see the New World if you don't
hustle and get going."

That was it for Zest.
We never got to boys.

CONNECTION TO RECOVERY

I was hurt and baffled, not only by JoAnn's mother's reaction, but by being unable to talk about it with my mother. Today, I know a loving parent would have asked me what was wrong. She would have said "I know you got a little enthusiastic, and maybe you over-reacted. But maybe something is going on with them that doesn't have anything to do with you. Would you like me to talk to JoAnn's mother? How can I help?" I can say similar words to my Inner Child when she is triggered

---

PROMPT:

1. Write about any time you lost a friend, particularly if you feel that you were somehow responsible for the situation.

2. What would you say to that friend today?

3. What would the former friend say to you?

4. Write a dialogue between the two of you. Begin it with "remember the time…" and write about the happy times with your friend.

Religious Abuse

We were Presbyterians before I turned ten in 1958. Church on Sunday was our only obligation. The Witnesses upped the ante. They required three meetings a week and knocking on doors proselytizing on the weekends. My father was violently opposed to the Jehovah's Witnesses – *Jehovees* —as he called them. He mocked them, swore at them. This only made my mother more convinced. I went along with my mother. My mother was my protector from my father. It never occurred to me to defy her.

But if I had felt different and not good enough before, living on a hardscrabble farm that was not a farm, isolated from friends, a failure at all sports, it got worse. I wasn't permitted to salute the flag or celebrate Christmas or my birthday. I was not supposed to associate with "worldly" kids. This was a form of religious abuse. I was forced to deny the normal longings of a ten-year-old. I was to behave like a "minister," converting people to a draconian religion. It wasn't long before I began resisting:

Converted

*I recall when I was nine -- the smell of wooden floorboards
in the ratty candy shop,
 the taste of Chuckles, crunch of sugar crust
 against the tongue, sticky gel caught in my teeth,*

*my bribe for sitting through the Reverend Kimball's
sermon.*

*I remember Sunday School, the golden rule, and making
dolls for little girls who didn't have a home.*

*I recall, when I turned ten, leather briefcases knocking
at my door, religion of salvation for the few; baptized
in a tub of water in the basement of the Kingdom Hall.*

91

*I remember Tuesdays, Thursdays, Sundays, scriptures,
strictures, adding up the hours in the tenements of
Trenton selling bible tracts, accounting for the cash.*

*I remember questioning why God would kill the babies
of Egyptians just because the Pharaoh held the Jews.
Why did God drown all the animals in Noah's flood
except the lucky two?*

*I remember thinking I was better off in Sunday School,
where God loved all the little ones.*

CONNECTION TO RECOVERY

I didn't have a choice about joining the Witnesses. In
that sense, I was a victim. Today, I can see the Witnesses
increased my sense of being different and not good
enough, feelings that created a great need for relief. My
experience of Jehovah as a God who made me do things
I did not want to do has definitely affected my ability to
find a Higher Power in recovery. As you will see in the
section called "Finding a Higher Power," it took time for
me to learn to trust. But I know there is a Higher Power
and I'm not it. I know there is a spirit within me of love
and compassion. I know that writing and other creative
work harnesses that Higher Power. And I know that the
spirit of recovery in the rooms of AA, Al Anon, and ACA
is the Higher Power at work.

1.Think about the Bible stories or other religious stories you were told as a child. Imagine what questions you might have had or actually did have about the stories.

2.If you grew up in a family that thought they were better than others, how was that message communicated to you? How did your family pretend they were better than others? Who were the "not chosen" people, and how did you learn to recognize and judge them?

My mother was converted by a Witness named Dot. She was the opposite in temperament from my mother. My mother loved to laugh, play with kittens, make up funny sayings, wear brightly colored clothes. Dot was all serious—all Jehovah. I tried to imagine what my mother must have thought of Dot. Here is a poem where I imagine my mother's voice, trying to understand the appeal of the Witnesses from her perspective.

Dot

I'd never met a woman plagued
by such eternal earnestness.
Her tight-wound curls a testament:
Jehovah despises outer beauty.

Her Naugahyde bookbag--
testament to "not like us."
I'd sooner buy leather second-hand
than flaunt the shiny seams of cheap.

Dot knocked on the back door of my brick farmhouse,
noticing I'm sure that the front door was obscured
by a pile of rocks. Dick said he planned
to build front steps. He never got beyond piling
up the battered stones.

93

I don't know why I let her in, except
that anyone who took the trouble
to risk the brambles on our lane, anyone
who had to say something that important,
well, I'd hear her out.

She held a Bible, asked if she could read
a verse. I'm sure I had a Bible somewhere, but
Bible-reading wasn't part of my routine. Salvation,
if it was coming, would require Dick to quit the booze,
a better job, a house with a front door.

Next week, she was back. This time with a book
and a proposal: how about a Bible study?
The study questions were printed
at the bottom of the page.

Dot was predictable. Someone I could count on.
I read ahead. I figured out the answers.
Next I knew, I was on a bus to a convention at Yankee
Stadium—40,000 Witnesses. Then another bus to Long
Island Sound with over 7,000 new recruits.

In my one piece suit and bathing cap,
I waded into the waves, found a "brother" in a white
tee shirt to gently dip me backwards in the sea.

Now I had a reason to get off the farm. Now I
had somewhere to go, with an urgent message:
The End is Coming. Join Us or You'll Die.

Dick's empty bottles gathered dust. The stones
languished at the front door. Now I had something
important to do—saving someone else besides myself.

PROMPT:

1.Consider anyone from your childhood who represented a serious responsibility, an upholder of rules, and write a poem about him or her. It might be a teacher, a minister, or other authority figure. See if you can explore that person's appeal.

2.Try writing dialogue between yourself as a child and someone in authority, a teacher, scout leader, sports coach. Have them try to convince you to do something you don't want to do.

Jehovah's Witnesses, young and old, were expected to go door to door with the Watchtower and Awake magazines, trying to convert people. This added a new humiliation. Sometimes I had to stand on a street corner holding up the magazines, which was terrifying as a young teenager, as I was literally asking people to look at me. We stopped for a treat on the way home. I see today I was being bribed.

Five Corners

*In Trenton, five roads converged
into a star. Which means,
if you are witnessing for The Truth,
if attracting crowds is what you want,
Five Corners is preferable to four.*

*That's where I was stationed, holding up
the Watchtower and Awake,
knowing I should engage with passersby,
spark a conversation about salvation and Jehovah.*

*Eyes on pavement, I stood, a human
poster board, hoping they would all pass by.*

*Five Corners, five streets of inner city
souls hustling to somewhere.*

*While on my mind,
 not their salvation,
not even mine,
but the banana Fudgsicle
 I'd get to suck on
after this was done.*

I particularly resented giving up Christmas. Until I was ten, Christmas was celebrated with a tree and gifts. I recall driving into Princeton to see the Christmas lights on all the houses. Those were magical times. I found a photo of what must have been the last Christmas we celebrated before my mother converted. I'm sure she was exhausted, trying to keep three children happy in an unhappy house. I wrote a pantoum about what I imagined her feeling:

The End of Santa

My mother looks disconsolate,
like crumpled wrapping paper.
Not what she got, not what she wanted,
not what she was hoping for.

Like crumpled wrapping paper,
as if she knew what was coming,
not what she was hoping for.
Next year, she'd no longer celebrate.

As if she knew what was coming--
her final Christmas Day. No Santa
Next year, she'd no longer celebrate
with cookies, gifts, good cheer.

Her final Christmas Day. No Santa.
Converted to Jehovah's Witnesses.
No cookies, gifts, good cheer--
she'd exchange them for The Truth.

Converted to Jehovah's Witnesses.
The coming war of Armageddon.
She'd exchange them for The Truth.
Convert her hapless children too.

The coming war of Armageddon.
Plaid-skirted on her chenille bedspread.
Convert her hapless children too,
looking woebegone and lost.

Plaid skirted on her chenille bedspread,
oblivious to the coming loss of hearth.
Looking woebegone and lost, the cookies
left for Santa on a small white plate

PROMPT:

1.Find a family photo from your childhood that stirs a
memory of conflicted feelings. Write down one of those
feelings and circle around it in the form of a pantoum.

2.Write about any holiday you can recall. See if you can
capture the fun of a special day. Write about your parents or
other caregivers and how hard they worked for you to have a
nice holiday.

Those of us raised in a religious tradition were generally exposed to prayer. Sometimes it was in church. Sometimes it was before meals or at bedtime. What was your experience? What did you pray for? Can you recall when you stopped those prayers (if you did?). As Witnesses, we prayed at meals, prayed in services, prayed at bedtime. But I honestly don't recall that we ever prayed for anything that felt important, such as for my father to stop drinking or be restored to sanity. In recovery, this is often the first thing we pray for—for help in putting down the drink or other addiction. This poem uses a form that starts with a full line and then begins the second line with the second word of the first line and so forth. Often a "repeating" form can help you explore the repeating nature of your past, those things you kept doing over and over expecting different results.

We Must Have Prayed for Something

Must have prayed for something, we
Have prayed for something, we must
Prayed for something, we must have
for something, we must have prayed
Something we must have prayed for.

If we believed God heard us
We believed God heard us, if
Believed God heard us, if we
God heard us, if we believed
Heard us, if we believed God
Us, if we believed God heard

No God or not the way he operates
God or not the way he operates, no
Or not the way he operates, No God
Not the way he operates, no God or
The way he operates, no God or not
Way he operates, no God or not the
he operates, no God or not the way
operates, no God . . .

CONNECTION TO RECOVERY

When I was little, prayer was a rote exercise. I was aware God failed to change things. As an adult, I do not believe that God grants prayers for what is called "intercessory aid:" heal the sick, stop a war, get someone a job. The ending of the poem with "no God" echoes this feeling from childhood. But I do believe in aligning my heart and mind with the love and compassion of a Higher Power. Often, my prayers are simply a person's name. I hold up their name in a sacred way to a Higher Power. My minister years ago said: "prayer doesn't change things. Prayer changes people," which I understood to mean me. That is the power of prayer.

Death of Parents

Sometimes, we are obsessed with someone who has died, someone we can no longer speak to. We may feel we have amends to make or that we need to express some hurt or realization to that person. When I was a senior in college at Berkeley, my dad was found unconscious in a parking lot behind a bar in Trenton, New Jersey. In the following example, I explore both my father's death and my mother's reaction.

John Doe 43

A dingy heap of denim work clothes
behind Sensi's Bar and Grill,
a gin mill with no juke box, dart board --

just the basics: dim lights, shots and beer.
As Jackson and Loretta angled for a parking spot,
she thought she saw the clothing tremble,

then collapse. Jackson was halfway in the door
when Loretta yelled, "My God! It's a man!"
His head was bloody at the back where he must

have hit the concrete, his pockets filled with
crumpled ones. He smelled like silage.
It didn't seem to be an accident, according

to the cop who finally came, probably a bar-room
brawl turned ugly in the lot. No one
seemed to know his name or where he lived.

Princeton General named him John Doe 43.
No CSI searched for weapons, missing persons.
Dusting for fingerprints seemed pointless.

Finally, they found my mom, demanded
that she pay the bill. He was cremated by the state.
His ashes came home in a cardboard box.

CONNECTION TO RECOVERY

My dad died destitute, homeless, and estranged from
his family. This is the alcoholic death we often hear
about. My mother's feelings were conflicted, as she
never received any child support and was
understandably upset that the hospital would ask her
for money. I felt caught "in between," a familiar feeling
for an Adult Child. I grieve for my father by telling his
story. I show compassion for my mother. I adopt my
father's alcoholic "bottom" as my own, reminding
myself that I cannot safely drink. I believe today he is
healed and has become one of my spiritual guides.

The following poem makes it sound as if the letters from my father were of similar value to his broken coffee cup. However, I realize how blessed I am to have letters written to me when my dad was apparently sober. Many of us in recovery have broken relationships with family who have died and nothing of the person to treasure what was lovable about him or her. But through writing, we can imagine that treasure is ours.

What's Left

The letters my dad wrote me
from the Walker Gordon Dairy:

I won the spelling bee when I was ten.
The word was Raspberry.
Tell that old battle-axe of a mother
of yours I miss her.

A cracked coffee cup—
the one he stored on the sill
above his bunkhouse bed

ONNECTION TO RECOVERY

Despite his alcoholism, my dad wrote to me in college.
He was thinking of me, proud of me. He was more than
his disease, as we all are. I invented the line about him
missing my mother and calling her a battle-axe, which
struck me as endearing. My father had a way with words.
He wanted to be a writer. I believe I am living that
unfulfilled promise for him.

PROMPT:

1.Write about what you have left from an important
person who died. Write about things. If you have
none, make them up or write about what you wish
you had but do not.
2.Imagine a letter from a parent who has died.
What would it say? Try to write concrete objects,
such as dishes, furniture, or photographs. You can
let these items stand as symbols for other dialogue
in the voice of that parent.

My mother also died young. She had a mastectomy at the age of forty-three and died when she was fifty. Her funeral was on my thirtieth birthday. For the last few years of her life, I returned to the east coast from law school in California, got a job in Manhattan, and spent weekends with her in New Jersey. I found instructions for her funeral on a yellow legal pad after her death.

Funeral Instructions

While I'd been sashaying
down Telegraph Avenue, hips swinging,
syncopated to the Rolling Stones,

bra-less beneath my leather jacket,
my mother had been lying on a metal gurney,
clammy to the touch, lips gray, not knowing

she'd awake to find herself one-sided.
I flew home. She wanted me to witness
the unveiling of her bandages.

The scar ran like a ragged river across her chest.
I said it didn't look so bad. Pills lined up
like foreign coins. They bought us seven years.

CONNECTION TO RECOVERY

Grief work requires that we talk and write about losses in our life. This poem reveals my sadness that my mother and I did not talk about her impending death. Although I tried to pretend that she believed she would recover, my mother knew she was dying and planned her funeral. She wanted red geraniums. I found them. And I've planted them for over forty summers in memory of her.

PROMPT:

1. Write about the death of someone close to you.

2. Write about someone who died where you were not fully present. For many in AA, we regret not being emotionally and physically present to loved ones when they needed us because we were drinking.

3. Write funeral instructions in the voice of someone who has died.

During those seven years, we took two trips to Europe together. Our second one was to Spain. Here I use the metaphor of how time is required to mellow black olives for the process of grieving and accepting death.

Given Salt, Given Time

I.

Before I knew what burrowed in her skin
would claim my mother's life at fifty-two,
leach out exuberance, her sass and flair,
strip hair from blonde to driftwood gray,

we holidayed in Spain, slipped into bars,
bought local wine, a meal with cheese and bread.
Aceitunas, olives, were required to turn
the commonplace to the sublime.

We feasted on their oily olive skins,
a soft resistance, ooze against the tooth.
We flicked our tongues against each fingertip,
licked the dripping oils, and sighed.

II.

That was before I knew what I know now,
that olives on the branch, grown full and lush,
will lose their clutch. They fall into the nets
below, still bitter and inedible.

Yet soaked in brine and stored in casks,
given salt and given time, the olives will turn
plump and savory as memory, a picnic
on a small Majorcan beach.

I was not able to grieve my mother's death for many years. Writing about our happy times helps me do that. My feelings about my mother are complex. Recognizing this helps me avoid black and white thinking. It also reminds me that I was present during my mother's illness.

PROMPT:

1.Find an object, like the olives in the poem above, that stands as a metaphor for the effect of time on the memory of someone you loved who has died.

2.Even if that person caused you pain, soften your eyes with compassion and put the two of you in a happy place.

3.Write to someone who has died telling them you regret not telling them you loved them or not being fully present.

Years later, I wrote a poem in a less narrative style about grief. You can see clothes hangers appear, as they will later in my poem about being left at secretarial school in New York City, knowing no one. You will find in your own writing that certain objects or images carry emotional weight for you. They will show up again and again in your work, reminding you that you have hit on something important.

What I Never Wanted

Ashes in a vase, September mourning,
distant calls of loons, a fractured sky,
sullen earth mounded under dogwood,
leaves burned hot as afterthoughts,

afternoon of unbelief, wall of windowpanes,
hangers in the closet, askew and bare,
their fragile chattering, a sound like empty acorns,
nutmeats dried, the harvest passed.

CONNECTION TO RECOVERY

This style of poetry requires emotional presence. By deleting a lot of the narrative detail that some readers insist on in order to "understand" the poem, I practice trusting the reader to get the feeling even if they have questions. Learning to trust has been a challenge for me because I didn't trust my parents to take care of me.

PROMPT:

1.Take a poem you have already written and convert it to a less narrative style, concentrating on words or images that carry emotional weight.

2.Begin a poem with "What I never wanted," or "I never wanted" and see where it takes you.

RETRIEVING HAPPY CHILDHOOD MEMORIES

Adult Children are often "black and white" thinkers. I cheat myself if I treat my childhood as all misery. There were happy times, times when my parents could be totally present and delight in each other and in me. Writing about them helps balance our grief. I resist the slogan, "they did the best they could," but I can view my childhood more gently if I accept that this may be true. I went through old photo albums and copied photographs that show happy times at the beach, or family picnics. I can see my parents delighting in me. I can revisit a time of happiness and wholeness.

I've kept my mother's wallet for forty years. It's stuffed with her credit cards, grocery coupons, old photos. Every once in a while, I take it out and touch my feelings.

What's Inside

my mother's wallet, worn red leather.
I've moved it from drawer to drawer
these forty years since she's been dead,
as if one day she'd show up at my door

headed for the grocery, needing
the coupons tucked inside,
as if she'd need my brother's photo
in his goofy glasses, back when he had hair,

as if she craved a whiff of leather
smell, before plastic took its place.
She'd gauge its bright red heft, back when
twenty bucks could see one through

a week. I've bought and tossed ten wallets
in these forty years, photos of my kids
replaced by licenses, credit cards,
twenty bucks now grown to two hundred.

Still, someday I may need what's
in this wallet, someday I may open it,
shake it inside out, hoping for a secret
left inside, a coupon for a double bonus life.

CONNECTION TO RECOVERY

Objects like my mother's wallet can link me to the past and remind me of the connection to those I loved. By writing about day-to-day events, such as shopping, I can capture some of the quiet, peaceful moments of my childhood, helping me avoid the black and white thinking that everything was chaos.

PROMPT:

1. Find an object that a loved one owned and write about it. Metaphorically "open up" the object and see what it reveals about that relationship.

2. Write about something concrete that you can use as a metaphor for someone you have lost, as I do with the coupons above.

My childhood was filled with raising dogs, cats, and even calves. My father loved animals. We raised black Labrador puppies to sell. He cared for them with joy. When we had a litter of kittens, he named each one for a racehorse. Watching the races on TV was one of our favorite Saturday afternoon treats. I recently came across a photograph of him holding a puppy under one arm and a pheasant under the other, looking pleased with himself. I also have photographs of him riding my grandfather's racehorses in the pasture. My father's rage and self-pity were calmed in the presence of animals.

Love of the Four-legged

When I was ten, we raised black angus calves,
dark-eyed, adoring as only beasts can be.
We named them Blacky, Blaze, and Joe.

At night, I'd trudge out to the barn with my dad,
lugging a metal bucket filled with steaming milk,
a giant rubber nipple sticking from its side.

Sometimes the calves broke free, escaped
into the neighbor's yard. My dad would collect
them in his woody station wagon.

Black furry faces peered from the rear window,
perplexed, like naughty children caught
telling jokes they didn't understand.

My father loved those calves
with pure uncomplicated joy,
reserved for the four-legged.

His heart beat pure in pastures.
They never asked for more
than he could give.

CONNECTION TO RECOVERY

Writing about the good times reminds us that we were lovable as children. My father had a longing for unconditional love, just as I did. He may not have been able to give that love to his children, but he was able to express it to animals. Animals, as I discuss later, can sometimes offer us the feeling of love we seek in a Higher Power.

PROMPT:

1. Think of a time when your parent or other caregiver was able to express affection, even if it was not for you. Write about it.

2. Think of any special gifts or talents your caregiver had and write about them.

3. Using the tool of compassion, is there an alcoholic in your life today who you can see in a new way? Write about that person in a scene where he or she is happy, joyous and free.

4. Experiment with enjambment, breaking your lines in unusual places. See how this affects your poem. Notice how in my last stanza I write "They never asked for more" and then continue on the final line: "than he could give." This is enjambment—when the sentence breaks and wraps into the next line.

My mother was contemptuous of my dad's alcoholism, but she was a naturally vivacious, beautiful woman who loved life. Despite embracing a strict religion, she loved to play and have fun. We played Scrabble, read Dickens together, went canoeing and traveled to Europe. Even after her mastectomy, she covered the bandage over her flat chest with flowered wallpaper to amuse her surgeons. She was an accomplished needlewoman who could knit complex patterns in a dark movie theater and delighted in making clothes for me, her only daughter. I have photographs of us in matching mother-daughter dresses. These items remind me that I was loved.

Outside the Frame

We are framed by wild roses,
wearing mother-daughter dresses
that my mother made –

green apples sway on white pique;
we squint into the sun, sandaled, tan,
in wait for some forgotten fete.

My mother could turn tissues
into a string of pink carnations,
dole out charm like Cheerios
spill into a breakfast bowl.

I wear her smile, catch her infectious
laugh, her love of brilliant clothes,
embrace the tiny thorns hidden
just beneath the blooms.

CONNECTION TO RECOVERY

Remembering how my mother showed her love for me helps me remember I am lovable and worthy. The tiny thorns in the poem evoke the dark side of pretty women, perhaps a sense of guilt over being too charming or flirtatious. There is both light and dark here, as in indeed, in all of life.

PROMPT:

1.Find good qualities about one or both parents and write about them.

2.Explore how you have inherited some of those good qualities.

3.Write about any special gift or funny family story involving one of your parents.

My home was chaotic and isolated. I read with envy stories about little towns with sidewalks. Then I found one of those towns – Spencer, Iowa, where my grandmother lived:

Spencer, Iowa

was a tidy Midwestern town
where my grandma lived –
with lakes, a candy store,
and an amusement park.

In Spencer, I fell in love with sidewalks.
I could follow sidewalks up and down
the blocks until I came to Julie's house.
She was an arranged friend – good enough
to last our two-week summer trip.

We'd sit in Julie's front room, slowly
turn pages of her Sears catalog,
find our favorite item on each page, imagine
who we'd be if we had all those treasures.

Sidewalks, Sears, houses close enough
to greet a neighbor in her yard, the taste of Tang,
the jingle of the ice cream truck, signposts
in a perfect pokey town.

CONNECTION TO RECOVERY
Capturing happy moments, particularly moments that evoke "home," remind me that I can create the feeling of home in my adult life. In finding a moment as simple as looking through a Sears catalog or tasting Tang, I remember that recovery is not a mountaintop experience. It is being able to enjoy being present in the moment.

1.Write about your idealized house, town, or life as a child. What would you eat? Who would be your friends?

2.Find an image (mine is sidewalks) that captures the essence of what you longed for as a child.

3.Write about a friend from childhood and some memory of having fun in a quiet moment.

As an isolated child, I spent a lot of time in my room, reading and listening to records. When I went to sleep, I turned on a New York radio station, WOR, and listened to the Jean Shepherd program. He told stories about small-town life. This was my lullaby, a soothing father's voice telling me stories. I would fall asleep to Jean and wake to the static that played after midnight sign-off. My record collection filled me with fantasy, but it also soothed my spirit and gave me a longing for connection.

Melodies

My record player spun a world of cocktail glamour,
of ice cubes' clink in highball glasses,

silky swish of satin skirts, flirts of saxophone,
toes twitching, hips itching, and laughter, always
laughter.

Jean Shepherd's lullaby, his voice on WOR
like milk and Oreos, chocolate flecks of gravel

in his voice, like sidewalks neat edged and precise,
smoothed like steps worn by penitents

waiting, waiting to light a candle, say a prayer,
to be counted as obedient, reflected in the glow.

CONNECTION TO RECOVERY

Jean Shepherd was the voice of the father I wanted. This poem reminds me that I found other voices to create safety and stability as a child. When I get stuck, I can remember Jean Shepherd. I didn't know my poem would jump from Shepherd to the penitents. That is the power of association.

PROMPT:

1. Write about a song from childhood that soothed you.

2. Write about the word "trust" and see what bubbles up.

CONNECTING CHILDHOOD WOUNDS AND LOSSES
TO CHARACTER TRAITS THAT IMPEDE RECOVERY

The first step in writing, as in working a recovery program, is to uncover the wounds and losses from childhood. We see that we are powerless over our childhoods. We take a searching and fearless inventory of our childhood experiences. Then we connect the wounds with our adult fears and behaviors. This is step 5 in the twelve-step program: "Admitted to myself, to God and to another person the exact nature of our wrongs." In AA, we say: "Alcohol was not my problem; it was my solution." We need to get down to "causes and conditions." Connecting our losses to our adult behavior is how we do that work.

AA uses the term "character defects" to describe personality traits such as being controlling, selfish, judgmental, or fearful. I've also heard these referred to in the Al Anon program as "isms," and as "character defaults." A character default is like a factory setting. If we stop working our program to change our behavior, we will revert to our original settings.

ACA says those who grew up in alcoholic or dysfunctional homes developed similar coping strategies, which infect their later lives and relationships. ACA has a list of fourteen effects of growing up with alcoholism. The word "defect" sounds harsh to many Adult Children. ACA calls them "traits." We did the best we could to survive. Our behaviors are not "mistakes." We couldn't have turned out any other way.

I will use the term Character Traits to describe the behaviors that many of us in recovery share. These include fear of abandonment and of angry people, people-pleasing, hiding our emotions (denial), becoming hyper-responsible and denying our own needs as we try to fix other people in an effort not to be emotionally abandoned. These Character Traits resulted from trying as children to control an uncontrollable environment. We are attracted to alcoholics for the same reason that we are attracted to drama and excitement: adrenalin makes us feel alive while at the same time avoiding focusing on ourselves and our needs. We walk on eggshells trying not to upset people we cannot please, yet we keep trying to earn their praise and affirmation to fill the emptiness within us. In an effort to superimpose the appearance of success, we become super-responsible, controlling, and deny our needs. Not surprisingly, we lose our sense of identity, feel we are wearing a "mask" and wonder who we really are.

Whether we are alcoholic, in a relationship with an alcoholic or had an alcoholic or dysfunctional parent, we share many of these fears and feelings and the resulting Character Traits.

Writing about our Character Traits helps us see that we have adopted behaviors that no longer serve us. It also helps us see that the person, place or thing upsetting us is generally a stand-in for a person, place or thing from the past. Hence the slogan: "when I'm hysterical, it's historical." When I can see that my reaction to the person in front of me is actually a result of my past, I gain the power to make a different choice today.

For example, I have an inordinate fear of anger and violence because of my childhood home. In my adult life, I noticed how this fear manifested when my daughter told me about a question her minister asked when she was preparing to be married. He asked her how her parents resolved disputes. My daughter said "well, I guess they go off and discuss them and come back and tell us the answer." What she was really saying is that she never heard us argue. Some might see that as the sign of a healthy marriage. I know it's because I will avoid an argument at all costs, fearing it will become so out of control that I will disappear or say something that will end my marriage. Walking on eggshells so as not to provoke an argument is not healthy. Saying "it's not so bad" or "how important is it?" is a way to talk myself out of telling my truth or standing up for myself. As I came to see these behaviors were the natural result of an upbringing in an alcoholic household, I can gently detach from them. They were needed to keep me alive as a child, but as an adult, they keep me from being in healthy and loving relationships.

As we work a program of twelve-step recovery, we begin to see our unhealthy Character Traits and realize that we have the power to change them. One way to uncover these traits and see how they have operated in our adult lives is to write about them. The following Prompts will help you uncover some of your Character Traits.

Fear of Abandonment or Being Left Out

I believe the central wound of childhood for most of us is fear of being abandoned—either physically or emotionally—and the resulting lack of trust. Our Character Traits were survival strategies to deal with this fear and lack of trust. The following poem imagines what is in my trashcan, which are literally items that are abandoned. The trash is a metaphor for the sense of loss and abandonment that led me as an adult to use alcohol as a "solution." Notice that the poem ends with a wine glass. I did not intend this image when I wrote the poem, before I began recovery. I realize now that I knew alcohol was hurting me even before I got sober.

This is an example of how poems reveal the writer's unconscious knowing.

Taking Out the Trash

Gritty coffee grounds
Crushed and wet
Release morning's breath

Grapefruit shell
Pink pungent taste
Small close compartments

Eggshell's jagged edge
Embossed with shiny film
No longer home

Ragged edge of newspaper
Curled into itself
Forgotten admonitions

A half-smoked cigarette
Lipsticked cherry red
A moist pink tongue

Broken wine glass
Slender stem intact
Aftertaste of loss

PROMPT:

1.Write about what is in your metaphorical trashcan, car, basement, attic or anywhere you keep unwanted items, or perhaps things you know you should discard. You can put people in there too!

2.Make a list of words with both strong sound and meaning that resonate with you. In my poem, the words "crushed," "jagged" "ragged" "broken" and "aftertaste" create a feeling of danger. Keep your word list and see where you can substitute those words for more ordinary ones in your writing.

The Bible is a treasure trove of stories that bubble up when I explore emotions of longing or disconnection. The following poem speaks to the fear of abandonment. It also involves issues of class, which tormented me as a child. It's the story of Ruth and Naomi. Naomi is Ruth's mother-in-law. Ruth, a foreigner, is married to the Jewish Naomi's son, Boaz. When Boaz dies, Naomi plans to send Ruth back to her homeland, which was the custom. Ruth pleads to stay with Naomi. I'm exploring contemporary notions of meddling mothers-in-law before turning the poem in a loving direction.

124

Mother-in-law

Just when you think you've heard enough,
her suggested hostess gifts, secret signals
of how her people learned to recognize each other,
the initialed cocktail napkins, pressed lightly to lips,
never mauled into a ball, a wrinkled mess.

Just when she starts in on the nursery
school, the kind where our kind
goes to get ahead,

Your head goes to Naomi, the Israelite,
mother-in-law to a heathen girl named Ruth.
Boaz, Naomi's son, stone dead, and Ruth, his widow,
lonely as the wind on Mount Moriah,

clings to Naomi's skirts, begs not be repatriated.
Ruth wants any task, just to hold the hand
of someone who once held him.
Wherever you go, let me go there too.

CONNECTION TO RECOVERY

We all have stories or myths that take root in our
subconscious. This story of possible abandonment had a
happy ending. Naomi let Ruth stay. This one reminds me of
the power of women in recovery. I need to keep them close
and ask for help, just as Ruth asked Naomi.

PROMPT:

1.Think of any story from the Bible, Shakespeare or any well-known piece of literature in which the characters display your longings or fear of abandonment. Transport those characters to a scene from your life and see what happens.

2.Write about any current conflict in your life and then "flashback" to a conflict in some myth or fairytale that relates.

After High School, when I went to secretarial school in New York, I experienced crushing grief and loneliness. Even though I wanted to escape from Jehovah's Witnesses back in New Jersey, I missed my mother and home. I felt socially awkward, unsophisticated, and fearful. In writing about it, I discovered an image of clothes hangers at the Barbizon Hotel, holding bathrobes my mother had made for me. The bathrobes were "making friends," as I was afraid I could not do in New York City.

Katie Gibbs School, 1965

The Barbizon Hotel, where I will live
while learning how to type,
echoes on this Sunday afternoon.

I clutch my bags, precise with items
on the packing list – it was suggested
I should bring a floor length bathrobe.

My mother made me two: an empire-waisted gown
of sky blue corduroy, punctuated with pearl buttons,
and one of moss-green flannel with a satin bow.

126

Soon I will be a secretary, work for a paycheck,
drink martinis with my boss in dimly lit restaurants,
buy a ticket to where I want to go.

But now, after my mother says goodbye,
I sink onto my single bed, engulfed by loss,
as if a wave has crashed and sucked me down.

My robes hang in my closet
chatter in excitement on their hangars,
as if they are already friends.

CONNECTION TO RECOVERY

By uncovering the feeling of abandonment as a young woman, I see how it has followed me from childhood. Today when my Inner Child is afraid of a new situation or feels "less than" in some way, I can invite her to tell me how she feels, assure her that she is lovable just as she is and that I will not leave her. I talk to her out loud (often in the car.) When she hears me say the words out loud, she believes me. The message that she is not alone is powerful. This is one way to "reparent" the Inner Child.

PROMPT:

1. Find an image, like the wave in this poem, that can stand as a metaphor for a feeling of abandonment you felt as a young adult. Then add another image, like the hangars, that can stand for hope.

2. Write a poem in which you plant dialogue of something you wish you had said or someone had said to you when you were feeling "less than."

3. Experiment with a "flash forward," as I do in saying I will soon be a secretary and drink martinis with my boss.

Shame

You would think that a child who grew up feeling shamed and shameful would strive mightily as an adult to avoid shame. But we often repeat conduct from our childhoods, unwittingly re-creating the environment we grew up in. As an adult, I managed to avoid the childhood feeling of lacking money and social prestige by becoming well-educated and getting a high-paying job. But the lack of self worth that led me into shameful behavior continued.

I attended college in Berkeley in the sixties—three thousand miles away from home, in an environment of lots of alcohol, drugs, and sex. I wanted to be an actress and was willing to disregard good sense to get on the stage, even performing nude on stage. This was part of my people-pleasing legacy from growing up in an alcoholic home. My dad came to Berkeley from New Jersey for a visit. I invited him to see my first role in the Magic Theater. I can't recall how I thought he would react to seeing me on stage in a nude football game. Did I want to shock him? He was frequently drunk, which I thought meant he lacked morals. Why was my behavior any worse than his? Plus, maybe he'd be too drunk to notice. Wrong. He made a scene in the middle of the show, stood up, hollered curses and stomped out of the theater.

Legacy

If he weren't drunk, would I have dared
display the body he had loved to life,

naked on a stage because it was the Magic
Theater, bare breasts my sole remaining trick,

a naked football game that shocked him to his feet
and out the door?

If he weren't drunk, would I have dared
to drink him two for two, then disappear into

a limerick with a man I'd met that afternoon,
when he who'd read me my first limerick

had left me, lost the right to shame me, his
shame the names of children on a court decree?

If I weren't drunk, would I have dared
to dare him shame for shame, defy him

to chastise me. Would I have dared collect
before his death on my inheritance?

CONNECTION TO RECOVERY

This poem uncovers the bravado that emerges when I'm
drunk. Both the conduct—playing nude theater—and
inviting my father to witness it were attention-getting
behavior. It also shows I didn't know my father very well.
I had confused his drunken rants and cursing with a lack of
morals, which was not the case. Note that I describe my
dad as the person who read me bedtime stories. There is
sadness in this poem, the loss of the "good dad" I missed as
a child.

Have you heard of "taking hostages" in recovery? To me, that means using my story, my power, my pain to draw another person into my vortex in an unhealthy way. In my past, I manipulated other people's sympathy the same way my dad did in my childhood when he pretended to have cut his foot and then showed us kids it was catsup. It also shows how I was addicted to drama as an attention-getting strategy.

Squirm

I squirm, remembering how I used
my father's death as my calling card,
slapped it on the table as if I'd earn
respect, as if I could force strangers to
smell the blood, the stink of silage,
the cloying sweet of Schnapps,
as if I'd transport them into the hospital,
feel the chill of his body, growing cold,
unclaimed, unnamed.

130

I've played my cards, king and ace.
"I've won," I want to shout, "You're done!"
But fingering their cards, ready for the
next hand, eager for their luck to change,
they ignore me and play on.

CONNECTION TO RECOVERY

I am addicted to adrenalin and to drama. I thought this dramatic story would make people feel sorry for me and like me. They may have felt sorry for me, but in an awkward, embarrassing way. It actually alienated them. I also see that I was genuinely grieving my father's death, but had no language for grief. I used the only language I knew – drama and chaos. Today, I can see the tragedy of his death and comfort my Inner Child who lost her father instead of expecting that comfort from strangers.

PROMPT:

1. Think of any time when you used a friend as a captive to a story of your pain. Imagine their reaction. Write a poem from your perspective.

2. Write a poem from the friend's perspective at the time.

People Pleasing

There is nothing wrong with wanting people to like us. But when we betray our true selves in trying to please or ingratiate ourselves with others, we are trying to get others to fill our emptiness. It doesn't work. And we lose our identity in the process. I wrote this poem in the voice of my mother. She taught me how to be pretty and how to flirt. This was people-pleasing behavior. I didn't know it could backfire. It seemed natural to me.

My Daughter's Birthday

Daughter, you begin your journey from a pool
where you've been floating to a light you can't imagine.

Soon enough I'll perch you in a tub of water on the grass,
posed for a Christmas card, naked cheer.

Until the water cools and life that requires rain,
an ancient incantation to conjure sun will usher
in uncertain scarcity.

You will lie, pretend, keep secrets, smile when someone's
watching, learn to love a dress with green apples, just
like mine, totter in my evening shoes, imitate my laugh.

And we will band together, pretty women, entertain
the men, despise their undersides, leave them in the
valley, windblown on our mountaintop.

CONNECTION TO RECOVERY

I notice how many of my behaviors were transmitted by my mother —both good and not so good. People-pleasing masked my True Self and made me feel like a fraud. I gave my power over to the people I was trying to please. Today my Inner Parent tells me that I am complete as I am. As a child, I was told by my grandmother, "You're not pretty when you don't smile." I don't need to smile when I'm unhappy or pretend to be self-sufficient when I need help. I can recognize the hurting Inner Children around me and reaffirm them, practicing the dialogue I also need to hear from my Inner Loving Parent.

My grandfather raised race horses, but didn't ride. Unlike my father, who would hop on a horse in the pasture and ride bareback, I was afraid of horses. I was skinny. They were huge. They seemed uncontrollable and immune to charm. But I wanted to please my grandfather, who arranged for me to take "riding lessons." Actually, he just put me on a racehorse and seemed to think I'd magically be able to ride. My people-pleasing kept me from voicing my fears. But a horse can smell fear from miles away.

The Scent of Fear

My grandpa named his racehorse after me,
a winner, hide as smooth as chocolate pudding,
pungent scent of barn and sweat.

He didn't ride but seemed to think I could.
At twelve, I was afraid of horses,
baleful eyes that seemed to size me up.

I mounted, sat astride 900 pounds of
pent-up boredom, mischief, or
simply aggravation. It didn't last.

133

It broke into a gallop. Reins swung
free, stirrups clattered at my knees.
Fixed to my saddle by the hope that maybe
it would change its mind, canter to a walk.

I hit hard-packed dirt, gritty in my mouth.
"I'll get back on. I'll get back on."
Struggling to my feet, I knew my lines.
And rode one time before I quit.

CONNECTION TO RECOVERY

The "fear inventory" in AA's step four showed me that I am
afraid of many people, places and things. Beneath the fear
is generally a feeling that I am not good enough to master
whatever the fear brings up. For example, I am afraid to
open a door to a recovery room if I've never been there
before and can't see inside. The feeling beneath the fear is
that I will be in the "wrong" room, everyone will look at me
and tell me I don't belong there. I can remind my Inner
Child that I will hold her hand and help her open the door.

PROMPT:

1.Write about a time you took a risk or did something you did
not want to do in order to please someone. What was the
result of this event?

2.Write about anything you are frightened of or write a list of
all the things you fear. Start with the easy ones, like snakes or
bees, and keep writing until you surprise yourself. Then write a
poem about the surprising fear.

Losing Our Identity

People-pleasing is one way we lose our identity, our True Self. As we conform our conduct to what we think other people want to see or hear, we ignore our own wants or needs. It's not uncommon to begin recovery with no idea of what makes us happy, what our gifts are, or what our true calling in the world might be. As we begin to explore our feelings we can see that even as children, we had talents and gifts. As a young person before recovery, I was attracted to the lives of other people that I found in books. Even as a child, I would hide from my father's anger with a book behind the drapes on a window seat. I can see that books were my parents for much of my life.

City Lights, San Francisco

Damp as a sodden bathing suit,
  beaches driftwood gray, fog obscured
  the Golden Gate, North Beach, Angel Island.

On Broadway, neon lights blessed a strand
of strip joints. The barker at the Condor Club plucked
my coat, urged me to try my luck in the topless contest.

Around the corner, I escaped to City Lights --
a bookstore bathed in shades of black,
home to Ferlinghetti, Ginsburg, Kerouac.

I wandered empty aisles, picked up a stack,
found a threadbare chair, settled into acrid pages,
searched a plot that I could fall into.

Even when I thought I was browsing in a bookstore, I was searching. I thought the "answer" to my loneliness and feeling alienated would be in a book. I wasn't ready to find the right "book" for many years.

PROMPT:

1. Write about any fictional character that you used as a role model when you were young and what qualities you wanted.

2. Think of a place, such as the City Lights bookstore in San Francisco, where you could "be yourself." Write about who that self was.

Fear of Standing Up for Ourselves

I avoid conflict, fearing anger and disapproval. If I stand up for myself, my Inner Child fears you won't like me and will leave. Here is a poem about a lie I told that had big consequences for someone in authority whom I wanted to please. Although the lie was couched as "standing up" for a professor accused of sexual manipulation, I should not have stood up for him. I should have stood up for the truth.

Stand Up

He was accused of lechery,
bragging about his hilltop orgies,
inviting students to come
and have some fun.

Had moans and shrieks, the shouts
of nameless couplings drifted down
the hill into the office of the Dean?

We knew our teacher's appetites were boundless.
In our drama class, he watched us squirm on the floor
acting like amoebae to the music of The Doors:
Come On Baby, Light my Fire.

He mounted his defense. Got us girls
together for the meeting with the Dean.
I replaced my miniskirt and clingy top
with an army shirt and jeans. Turned curls
to braids. Washed off my mascara.

" I've never seen the Professor do anything
 inappropriate." The others nodded.
Why lie? I knew he'd never cast me in a play.
He knew I'd never join his orgies.

The Dean saw we'd been well-rehearsed.
He snapped shut his briefcase,
withdrew.

CONNECTION TO RECOVERY

A first cousin of people pleasing is conflict avoidance. In order to refuse to lie for my teacher, I would have had to stand up to him and say what he was asking was wrong. I am still afraid to face conflict, even in sobriety. But I can discuss a conflict with a friend and work out what I will say. I am a reactor rather than an actor. Therefore, I want to have my defense or reply ready in an instant. I can pause when agitated. I can work on language that says what I mean, but not meanly. I avoid texting or emailing important messages. I recognize I try to hide behind technology. I need to practice face-to-face conversations.

PROMPT:

1.Write about a lie you've told in order to "help" someone. Imagine what you looked like before and after the lie. You will see in this poem I literally changed my clothes, but we change in more subtle ways too. Think about body language.

2.Write about the consequence of a lie. If you think there was no consequence, make one up.

3.Write from the perspective of the person you lied to. What would they say to you then? Today?

In my ACA meetings, we ask people to share a "success" at the beginning of each meeting. A common success among newcomers is in confronting an unacceptable situation and standing up for ourselves. As a people-pleaser, my default position when I am upset with someone is to wait awhile and then ask myself "how important is it?" Pausing is a good recovery strategy, but talking myself out of confronting another person is not. I ask myself the Al-Anon questions: Does it need to be said? Does it need to be said by me? Does it need to be said right now?

Here is a poem based on a "feelings exercise" in the ACA step workbook. It asks us to name a feeling and connect it to an event. If I discover strong feelings, I know I need to own my truth in order to become my True Self.

If Feelings Could Talk

I feel diminished when you act like you are listening to me but I know you aren't.
I feel angry when you are late.
I feel unimportant when I call you and you don't call me back.
I feel upset and frustrated when you tell me you don't like the way I talk to my grandchild.
I feel unappreciated when you ignore the gift I sent you.
I feel sad and hurt when you don't ask to read any of my writing.
I feel manipulated when you call me saying you want to know how I am but then talk only about yourself.
I feel helpless when I get in the middle of an argument you have with someone else.
I feel overwhelmed when I say yes to a project and then realize I don't have the time or skill to do it well.
I feel annoyed when I offer to organize something and then you don't like the way I did it and want to change it.
I feel impatient when you go on and on talking about things that I think are unimportant and I'm not interested in.
I feel irritated when you act like your problems are emergencies and I have to stop immediately what I'm doing and help you.
I feel embarrassed when you refuse to follow rules, like traffic lights or picking up dog poop.

When I see all the situations where I "stuff" my feelings or talk myself out of them, I can see that avoiding naming my feelings and talking about them keeps me from becoming my True Self. Everyone gets angry. Everyone feels scared, or hurt, or embarrassed. By avoiding asking the other person to change their behavior and by avoiding the "you always/you never" style of confrontation, but simply owning my feelings, I can defuse what may be minor annoyances or even misperceptions before they solidify into TRUTH.

PROMPT:

1. Write a list of all your current resentments, big and small. Then turn the resentment into a sentence beginning "I feel."

2. Try to find as many different words for feelings as you can. If you are someone who often feels angry, or guilty, or diminished, take a look at all the feeling words in the Appendix and use them, even if you think you never feel them.

Struggle Setting Boundaries

Al Anon says that I am powerless over another person's behavior. I do not have a choice to try to change them—simply because I can't change anyone but myself. If someone triggers me or makes me feel uncomfortable or if they engage in behavior I find unacceptable, I have three choices: 1. accept that person just the way they are, 2. decide not to have that person in my life, or 3. set boundaries on how and when I will engage with that person. There is great relief in this simple strategy. Unfortunately, if I am acting out my Character Trait of people-pleasing, I keep people in my life who are not good for me in an effort to get them to like me and avoid being emotionally abandoned. And this is true even if I am the one setting a boundary!

Setting boundaries is also hard because I am a conflict-avoider. I never learned how to express my feelings and state my needs. Therefore, I assume if I try to set a boundary, I'll either be speechless and cave in to unacceptable behavior or a huge fight will ensue.

Deciding that a sponsor-sponsee relationship is not working is a good example. Even when a sponsee is not keeping their commitments, I am reluctant to acknowledge that. I have a program friend who was afraid to tell her hairdresser she didn't like the way the hairdresser did her hair! That sounds silly, but I totally understand. I believe honest communication without anger or accusation is one of the most important tools in recovery and one that most of us never learned how to do.

Boundaries

The garden, edged with wire,
a jaunty scarecrow, a bit of coyote
urine, hair shavings from a buzz cut.

Don't call me, text me.
stop with the emojis, no more
cute animal videos.

I'm at the edge of nowhere,
on edge, waiting for silence,
flicker of senses, a sense of roots

growing underneath my feet,
threatening to expose themselves,
wrap around my ankles.

I'm afraid you will show up
with the kitchen shears
or a basket filled with bees

I've set a boundary to protect
the baby lettuce, a chance to grow
without withering or sunstroke--

fieldstone, sandstone, slate or granite
dragged into place, balanced
like a conversation resting on a sinkhole.

CONNECTION TO RECOVERY

It is unreasonable for me to expect that I will like everyone I meet and they will like me. It is unreasonable for me to expect that people will change based on something I say or do. I recently set a boundary with a woman friend who criticizes how I raised my daughters. I told her this hurt my feelings. I now see her on a limited basis. We have both accommodated to a different relationship.

PROMPT:

1.Write about someone you want to set a boundary with or someone who set a boundary with you. Write loving words that do not accuse but acknowledge your feelings and the limits you choose to set on the relationship.

2.Write about the fears you have if you set a boundary. It might be that you will never have another friend or that the other person will gossip about you. See what stands in the way of your setting boundaries. Find a concrete image, such as the baby lettuce in the poem above, that stands for that part of you that you feel you need to protect with a boundary.

Being Controlling

One of my Character Traits is being controlling. I am addicted to activity, packing in so many projects that I don't notice my feelings and live on the adrenalin released by the fear of not getting the projects all done right or on time. This both recreates the chaos of my childhood home and keeps me "busy" so I don't have to dwell on my behavior. I like schedules and routine. I'm not happy with free time and I often question what "normal" behavior is.

I know my parents passed certain traits to me and I have doubtless passed some to my children. Did I teach my children their worth came from their accomplishments? I hope not.

In the following poem, I tried to adopt the voice of a child who was bewildered by the jogger-strollers popular today. This contraption is a metaphor for how I may have disconnected from my children in my efforts to "get ahead." The baby in this poem couldn't see his mother yet he sensed she was nearby. That sense of confusion often affects our adult lives too.

Born to Run

I

*I'm dreaming of my mother's arms, so soft and white,
holding me to her chest, dripping from my bath.*

*then wrapping me in soft yellow towels, kissing
my toes. I love that. When she kisses my toes.*

*I'm dreaming of milk, only I don't know it's milk,
just that its warm and sweet and dribbles down*

*my chin. But lickety split, there comes a terry
bib to wipe it off. Another kiss. Feels good.*

I'm dreaming of drifting off into a nap.
The sun is sparkling on the shades she's

pulled so I can close my eyes. My mobile
circles slowly overhead.

||

I'm bundled up and bundled in.
My mommy's running but I don't know where.

Wisps of breeze drift by. I sniff her shampoo
smell. Birds skitter in the trees, then disappear.

The trees move by so fast. Just as one
starts to form a shape, it's gone.

We're running. My nose is running.
My nose is red and cold.

My toes are scrunched up
in little leather boxes with ties on them.

They aren't soft or warm. My toes can't breathe.
No one can find them to kiss them.

And furthermore, I'm hungry. I haven't learned
to tell time with a clock. I tell it with my tummy.

My tummy says Milk Now! But I don't know
the word for milk.

I'm learning. Learning how to wait.
Waiting for the day I get my running shoes.

In this poem I can relate both to the running mother and the confused baby. The baby at the end is waiting to get running shoes and become just like his mother! Yet, I can feel the baby's longing to slow down and be connected to the mother. This reminds me I can slow down in recovery.

PROMPT:

1.Find an object (mine was the jogging stroller and running shoes) that evokes a behavior you see as a multi-tasking—doing more at one time than you should do. Imagine you pass on this behavior in your family.

2.Write a poem in the voice of a child, or your Inner Child. Express your confusion about mixed signals you received as a child.

In the following poem, I make a play on words by titling the poem "Living in the Projects," a run-down tenement that no one would want to live in. Yet, by filling my mind and my time with projects designed to get me praise, am I not inhabiting a similar place? Once I truly see that there will never be enough praise from outside myself to fill the empty core of "not enough," I am free to choose projects that reflect my True Self, rather than a wounded Inner Child seeking approval.

Living in the Projects

It might as well have been a tenement,
stinking of piss and cooking cabbage,
the neighborhood I call my mind.

My projects were as plentiful as ants
at a summer picnic, mosquitos buzzing
at my pillow, the sound of fistfights
down the hall:

Become a Girl Scout Leader, Church
School Teacher, Organize Vacation
Bible School, Direct ten-minute plays
at Church.

Make costumes and fancy tidbits for
elementary school: Japan Night,
Africa Night, India Night.

Teach 4th graders how to type. Read
them Harry Potter.

Sew matching Easter dresses, prom dresses,
flower girl dresses, bridesmaid dresses.
Make maternity clothes.

Volunteer to lead the Poetry Society,
incorporate a nonprofit, become secretary,
treasurer, keeper of records.

Book Group. Poetry Group. Poets on Poetry
at the Library. Show up. Show off.
When will it be enough?

PROMPT:

1.Make a list of all the projects you have taken on that were not your job, but things you have volunteered to do that keep you moving, running, releasing adrenalin into your system.

2.Imagine that one or more of these projects backfires, as I do in the final stanza, revealing the danger in taking on too much.

Denial

Denial is a powerful survival strategy. It keeps us from feelings that we fear might destroy us. As we grow in recovery, feelings will return. We will retrieve memories. I saw how many times I denied my True Self, when my Inner Child was hurt or frightened, by resorting to platitudes or statements that minimized or denied my experience. When I came into AA, I believed I had one drink a day for years. But as I reviewed my past, I realized that I never had one drink. Sometimes I'd just top up my wine glass before it was empty, but that was not one drink. My grandmother would say at family parties, "Would you like a dividend?" Doesn't that sound lovely and polite? She really meant, "Do you want another drink?"

When someone asks me how I am and I reply, "fine," that is not always true. With some people, it's not appropriate to reveal all my feelings. But in program, I need to recognize and verbalize my feelings if I want

147

to grow. Recently, someone asked me on a cold, wet spring day how I was doing. I said, "Drizzly." He knew just what I meant!

Finding those phrases that we use to deny our true feelings is a good way to write about denial.

Denial

I'm fine. Really fine.
Her criticism didn't bother me.
Those weren't really tears.
I'm fine. Really. Fine.

It didn't hurt that badly.
It was clear he'd changed his mind.
We get to fall in love and out.
It didn't hurt that badly.

Other people have it worse.
The mothers who can't feed their children.
The refugees in camps.
Other people have it worse.

What's past is past.
I say let bygones be bygones.
Put one foot forward and march on.
What's past is past.

CONNECTION TO RECOVERY

When I hear the things I say, either out loud or to myself, I can see the extent of my denial. Then I can start to tell the truth about how I really feel, recognizing that my feelings may change, but I can express them in the moment. If I am overly agitated, I can pause and ask whether I need to express a feeling right now. But I need to be cautious that I don't wait and then talk myself out of my feeling after it has passed.

1.Think of the phrases you say when someone asks you how you are. Write about what you say and what you would say if you were telling the truth.

2.Write about phrases you recall from childhood that caused you to deny your feelings. This is a good way to identify the voice of the Inner Critical Parent and to see where you repeat it today.

3.Write about any old statements you used to say to yourself that you do not say today, or write what you would like to say instead.

Using Sex to Manipulate and Avoid Being Abandoned

As a Berkeley student, I often got into uncomfortable situations with men. As a people pleaser, I did not consider saying "no" or "stop." I thought there was something wrong with me that I seemed to attract men who saw me as a sex object. I now realize that in my desire for attention, I was sending out mixed-signals with my clothing and my flirtatiousness. This was partly because I was addicted to the excitement of a new relationship. When added to my trait of people-pleasing and fear of abandonment, I was often baffled how "I got in this situation again." Now I know.

I romanticized my many boyfriends, but the truth was that I was more than willing to fall for any man who paid attention to me. My dad visited me in Berkeley, got drunk and entertained two of my boyfriends. This bizarre evening somehow seemed normal to me.

The Contenders

My wild Armenian, hitchhiked around the world,
screwed a hundred girls, each one replaceable, 'til he met me.
When he declared he'd cut his arm to prove he loved me
more than them, I wanted him to do it.

My Chicano, an aspiring politician, made me wish I'd been
born brown. Masquerading as his campaign worker,
I feasted at fiestas on tortillas and tamales,
learned the rhythm of a mariachi band.

One night my father came for dinner. A dozen roses graced
the dining table – the card was blank. One man and then
the other showed up at the door. The roses urged us "eat,
drink," spilled scent like wine in our laps.

One man knew he'd sent them. Both kept their peace.
As tension mounted, they found release in swapping stories
with my father -- the pampas, politics, their past.

Finally, I went to bed amidst the buzz of drunken laughter,
calculating how long I'd get to keep them both.

CONNECTION TO RECOVERY
I thought that dramatic situations like this just "happened" to me, but I must have invited both men to dinner. I need to acknowledge my part in order to have authentic relationships today. Today my Inner Loving Parent can remind me that healthy people love me for myself. I do not need to create dramatic situations in which I am the star.

My version about how many of my relationships ended is that we just "drifted apart." Actually, there was no drifting. I manipulated and engineered almost every relationship.   And I always had the next relationship lined up before I manipulated the current man into leaving. It took me years in recovery to see the depth of my denial and the extent of the pain I caused other people.   As you can see in Bridalveil Falls, I created drama and I was a manipulator.

Bridalveil Falls

In a meadow in Yosemite, I'm zipped
into a deep green sleeping bag
with a man I know I'll never marry.

The dew sparkles on yellow mountain flowers
as sunlight on Half Dome Mountain to the west hints

151

at the warmth that will wake him in ten minutes.
Bridalveil bathes granite boulders in their mist, tadpoles
teem in craters filled with snowmelt, tiny incandescent
squiggles like clippings from fingernails.

Perfect for a honeymoon.

But there's another man waiting in the city. As if a handful
of fish food has been tossed into a koi pond
a struggle churns below the surface.

The camping man awakes, unaware the prince appeared
while he was fast asleep.

CONNECTION TO RECOVERY

I ended up in Yosemite because my former boyfriend showed up at my apartment where I was living with my next boyfriend and "kidnapped" me. Did I go willingly? I did. He counted on my addiction to drama to convince me to go. I can create drama in my daily life, for example by gossip. I can insert myself into other people's dramas by offering advice instead of simply listening. Whenever I find myself obsessing over a person, place, or thing, I should ask myself if that obsession is feeding drama. Drama is not healthy for me.

PROMPT:

1. Write on the topic of "true love."

2. Write a piece using "Prince" or "Princess."

3. Choose some images to write a poem about a failed love relationship. It could be yours or someone else's. Often we can see our relationships more clearly in the mirror of others' relationships.

Thinking back, I realize that I had a number of close calls to being assaulted or raped. Many of them I had "forgotten" until I started writing these poems. The following poem resulted from a Prompt to think of something ugly or bad that happened to me and to write it from the perspective of what I "loved" about it, using a breathless style of run-on sentences joined with "and."

Under Spanish Skies

I loved the song by ABBA, Fernando
sung in English, although they were Swedish
and they didn't speak in English,
and I loved the bartender,
who spoke only Spanish. It didn't
matter to Fernando, because the song
was ABBA and you could dance
to it in any country, and I loved the taste
of the red wine, kind of vinegary with
licorice, and I didn't know its name.

And I loved how there was Paolo
and how I knew that was his name from
the tag on his shirt at breakfast, but
this wasn't breakfast, it was near midnight,
and I loved his black shirt and tight trousers,
a kind of uniform, and I loved how Paolo
was probably younger than I was and was a good
dancer and how he twirled me around the floor,
brought me back with one hand on my back,
and as he didn't speak much English, I didn't
need to talk to him, but ABBA was still playing
and I loved how another drink appeared
on the small glass table, and how Fernando
was still playing.

And I loved Paolo's black eyes
that matched his shirt and I could tell
he remembered me from breakfast because
he was so friendly, so courtly and well-mannered
like a Spanish gentleman, and how he asked
if he could walk me back to my hotel
and I loved that he knew a shortcut up a dirt hill
and there were all those Spanish stars, and I loved
how

154

he swung me to him at the top and pulled me
in a rough hug which wasn't like dancing
to Fernando.

And I loved the fear that shot up my spine
like I'd plugged my hair dryer into a foreign
outlet and how when I looked around,
we were totally, utterly and obviously alone.

I loved how when I said
the universal word for "No," which is "No,"
he laughed. And I loved the moment of
the standoff, when he considered if I
was worth losing his job for. I loved
learning that I wasn't worth it.

CONNECTION TO RECOVERY

I see this event as a moment to feel gratitude that it didn't end badly. I acknowledge "my part" by realizing that I was drunk and feeling the immunity from danger that drinking can create. By writing in a breathless style, I get to see how I set myself up for that walk by my romantic fantasies.

PROMPT:

1.Write about a sexual situation that may have seemed minor at the time, but which strikes you today as being more significant. Use the idea of piling one detail on top of another with as much specificity as you can, avoiding "telling" the reader about your thoughts now. Let the narrative unfold.

2.Write about any situation where you manipulated someone into doing something. Think of all the "good reasons" you told yourself and write about them in this run-on style.

I started thinking about Monica Lewinsky, the White House intern who was sexually involved with Bill Clinton. I heard her mother when interviewed complain, "why is it always called the Lewinsky scandal? Why not the Clinton scandal?" There are many answers, including blaming the victim. And of course there was not just one Clinton scandal. Lewinsky has since become an articulate anti-bullying advocate. She has never said that Clinton forced her or overpowered her. In fact, I heard her say in a TED talk that she "fell in love with my boss." But he was charismatic, the most powerful man in the world. Power is sexually alluring. I recognize that I, too, have been seduced by the sexual power of men in authority. I wrote this poem from the standpoint of "relate and don't compare," which showed me that Monica Lewinsky and I were not all that different at 21.

What I Would Say to Monica Lewinsky

I think about you
when I close my eyes
fantasize about the intersect
of power and attraction,

when I'm in a flash-back,
envisioning me as twenty-one again,
full fleshed and pink lipped.

I told myself you were dumb,
naïve, nubile, an adventuress,
took advantage of the beret
and what you knew of appetite.

They didn't make thongs back then,
when I was on the prowl.
But who's to say if I'd had the chance,
I wouldn't have worn a see-through
blouse, sent a perfumed thank-you note?

Being a people-pleaser, being addicted to drama, and seeking the adrenalin high of a sexual chase are all Character Traits of the Adult Child. I see compassion for myself in this poem, recognizing that before recovery, I might have simultaneously blamed myself as an adventuress and tried to seduce an older man, as in fact I did with a college professor. (I'm grateful he was immune to my see-through blouse.) I was desperate for attention. Today, my Inner Loving Parent tells me: "you are worthy of intimacy just as you are. You have something loving and beautiful to offer."

PROMPT:

1. Put yourself in any sex scandal in the news. There are plenty to choose from. Imagine what you would have said or done before recovery.

2. Write what you think Monica would like to say to Bill Clinton today.

3. Clinton was asked if he has apologized to Lewinsky. His answer waffled. Write a complete apology from him to her.

I recall years later being offended when a friend gave me a vase for my birthday inscribed with the words "Ashes of Dead Lovers." She thought it was funny, not knowing just how many "dead" lovers there were. I was appalled, and couldn't conceal my reaction. She handed me the receipt and I returned it for a soap dish

Ashes of Dead Lovers

The vase engraved: Ashes of Dead Lovers.
Amazed, enraged, her birthday gift arouses
my defense of each specific man –

scent of his skin, the shape of fingernails,
what he found funny, what seemed fierce,
the part of him I loved the most,

now debased, each man's sweet particularity
commingled in a common grave.

CONNECTION TO RECOVERY

These events uncover amends to make. I have made
amends to many of the men I used and discarded in my
younger days. You will see some poetry prompts on this
topic under the heading "Amends" later in this book.

PROMPT:

1.Write about your first love, what you expected and what you got.
Who broke up with whom? Are you still in touch? Imagine you find
him (or her) on Facebook today. If you look for clues that he hasn't
forgotten you, what would those clues be?

2.Imagine the person with whom you are in a relationship today
comes across a letter an old lover wrote you, or a text between you.
Imagine something in the message changes what your lover thinks
about you or what you have told him (or her) about yourself.

3.What person have you treated most shabbily? Write that person's
poem about YOU. What would that person say? Imagine he sees a
wedding announcement or that you have won an award, or that
you've been arrested for drunk driving or embezzlement. How does
this change the poem?

Fear of Anger and Chaos

Many of us grew up in chaotic households with violence and the roller coaster of unpredictable events and responses. This is drama. It released adrenalin in our young bodies. That adrenalin helped us remain vigilant so we could survive. Unfortunately, in adult years we often seek out people or situations that will mimic that drama so that we can feel "something." For us, feeling the adrenalin rush is preferable to feeling numb. We are often attracted to angry people, even though many of us fear anger. We sometimes act out anger to produce adrenalin. The following is a form of poem called a "rant," a list of all the things you are mad about. It helps to get the anger out on paper.

Manifesto of the Sick and Tired

I'm sick of kale, quinoa, and soy milk, tired of talk
about digestion, the movements of a masticated mess,
its slow progression through the bowels, the need to cleanse.
I will not be cleansed.

I hate panty lines and the party line, sound bites,
politicians who flash their johnsons on the internet but claim
they can control themselves in times of crisis, debt, destruction
or decision. I'm tired of gridlock, focus groups, splinter groups
my tax dollars at work, or not. I'm sick of filibusters.
I will not be filibustered.

I'm tired of Facebook, Smartbook, of being linked in and looked at.
And I'm sick to death of the Kardashians, a plumped up exfoliated
tribe who, a hundred years after their ancestors were marched
across Armenia as slivered shadows, have morphed into it-never-
happened, who thrive on plastic surgery and an excess of
consumption.

I will not be consumed.

I'm sick and tired of hearing there's not enough to go around. I'm tired of No Child Left Behind, children left in burned out buildings, kids left in steaming cars, kids who step on needles in the park. I'm sick and tired of us and them and them and them.

I will not be us. I will not be them.

CONNECTION TO RECOVERY

The idea of "them and us" reminds me that I can be judgmental, assuming "they" are wrong and I am always right. Even when my anger is justified, I ask myself if it's my business to wade into the battle.

PROMPT:

1.Write a rant. Write about all the people, places and things that stir you up. Don't try to shape the poem at first.

2.You will see that eventually I came up with the idea of "I will not be..." You can look over your poem and impose some order on it. Repetition of a word or phrase is a form of order too. Order helps control angry outbursts.

Being Rescuers

Wanting to rescue other people stems from traits we learned in childhood: being super-responsible, controlling, and always having an exit strategy. I am an excellent problem solver. Unfortunately, many people don't want me to solve their problems. They want me to listen to them and hold their pain gently. This makes me feel uncomfortable, as I don't like to experience pain—mine or others'. I thought about all the "helpful advice" I've given, particularly to my spouse and children and came up with this List Poem:

The Rescuer

10 helpful hints to make you a better person

I just had an excellent idea –
When I was your age, I never –
If you start saving now, by retirement—
I read only yesterday, kale is the new—
You'd be so much happier if you only –
Is <u>that</u> the guy you're throwing yourself away on—
They say a masters' degree correlates with increased—
If you were to say "I'm sorry," first –
Do you think that shirt brings out your best –
Sweetie, Facebook is not your friend.

CONNECTION TO RECOVERY

In Al-Anon and ACA, we say "we do not give advice." It's good to remember that when I give advice, I am often like the director spoken of in Alcoholics Anonymous who tries to run the entire play.

PROMPT:

1.Think of all the advice you have given to others, whether they asked for it or not. Make a list of some of the things you said.

2.Turn all the advice you gave others around to yourself. Can you take your own advice? Write a poem about the experience of turning your advice around or what you learned doing so.

3.Imagine a past situation in which you gave advice. Write about what the situation might have looked like if you had withheld advice. Write about listening – how it feels to listen without giving advice, what you'd say, what's different.

I wrote a poem using the lyrics from a sixties song called "Rescue me." From my earliest writing in recovery, song lyrics have helped me shape my poems and unlock hidden meanings.

Rescue Me

Rescue me, and
Take me in your arms

'Cause my snow fort has collapsed
and I've got a frozen heart
Dig me out.
Only you can thaw my icy part.

Rescue me.
I want your tender charms.

Like a snake shut up for years
in a genie's battered vase
blow your melody, remove my fears
coax me with your fearless gaze

Rescue me
Cause I'm lonely

It's midnight in the neighborhood.
All the windows shuttered tight.
Tell me I'm unique, that I'm enough
Tell me everything will be all right

Rescue me
And I'm blue

midnight blue. Ocean-covered wrecks blue.
Drunk-eyed blue. No out within a shout
blue. Low down, ain't nobody around blue.
Turn me upside down. Turn me inside out.

Rescue me
I need you

Only you will do. Endlessly inventive.
Every good idea begins and ends with you.
Write my lines. Set the scene. Light me up.
I have no idea what I'm supposed to do.

So Rescue me
And your love too.

Lie to me. Lie and say you love me.
Engulf me in your superiority.
I'm worthless without your cleverness.
Come on. Rescue my inferiority.

CONNECTION TO RECOVERY

I can be both the person wanting rescue and the person believing I am the savior and rescuer. I need to remind myself that I am not responsible for anyone's happiness but my own. One reason I lapse into rescuing is because I become convinced that I know what is for the best. When I trust in outcomes and consider the possibility that my idea might not be the best outcome, I can become an actor rather than a reactor.

1.Imagine that you are asking to be rescued from a relationship, a job, a financial problem. Write about all the ways you would try to get someone to help you.

2.In this poem, you will see that the narrator is telling the rescuer that she is worthless without him. Write about any time the idea of needing another person to give meaning to your life cropped up.

3.Write about a time you rescued someone else. Describe all the ways you attempted to help the other person and how that felt. Was there any cost to you or the other?

Acting as Victims

I did not instantly relate to being a victim when I came into the ACA program. I defined a victim as someone who complained all the time, blamed other people for her problems and was "needy." I didn't feel like a victim because I had career success and no one was forcing me to do something I didn't want to do. But then I found a new definition of victim: someone who believes they have no choices.

I made choices in changing jobs, but in my marriage, I was stuck and acted as if I had no choice. My husband is an introvert. He is also an Adult Child who prefers to isolate. But when I met him in the office, he had been an out-going, life-of-the-party kind of guy. I thought if I just found the right group of friends or fun activity, he would turn back into that charming man. I didn't realize that he was wearing a mask at work, that his True Self was depressed and without joy. I kept doing the same thing over and over expecting different results.

In all my years of complaining about being married to a hermit or telling "funny" stories about him, it never occurred to me that I could leave. When we married, I was convinced that if I didn't marry this man, I would never get married. I'd been engaged when I was eighteen, but that collapsed before we seriously discussed marriage.

None of the men I'd been in serious relationships with from age twenty to thirty ever proposed. In truth, my husband didn't propose either. We discussed marriage with a yellow legal pad of "pros" and "cons."

So no. I didn't think I had a choice. And in that respect I've been a victim. Now that I can see clearly who he is and what he can and cannot do, I do have a choice. I can accept him as he is, set boundaries in our relationship, or leave. But here's one choice I do not have: I do not have the choice to change him.

As I thought more about being a victim, I realized that I had no choice over my parents, my dad's alcoholism, my mother becoming a Jehovah's Witness. I wrote a poem to "own" my lack of choices. Here, I acknowledge some of my childhood losses as if I were a victim.

In the Land of Victimhood

> *I wish I'd had:*

a better dad
one more like Mr. Rogers with his neat brown cardigan, his tennis shoes, his calm measured voice, and puppets living in a made-up neighborhood.

a better car
a Mercedes or a Cadillac--not our beat up woody station wagon that smelled like the calves we hauled back when they trotted off to the neighbors' yard.

a pony
a better pony than the one I had--that snapped at you, knocked you off the saddle, and dragged you down the lane.

the ability to add

instead of having to rely on my fingers. Scrabble would have been a
snap if I could have predicted the score before I laid down my tiles.

a bit of Proust
so I could hold my own at dinner parties talking with erudition about
madeleines, their triggers of the memories I long suppressed.

a dancing partner
 a man who would take me in his arms, gaze at me the way Barack
looked at Michelle at his inauguration ball.

a steady eye
to hit the ball--the tennis ball, the softball, ping-pong, even the
croquet ball, all those balls that slipped away when I clenched my
eyes instead of honing in on their direction.

It seemed I had no choice--
I was destined to wear hand-me-downs, suck at sports
get a dad who broke the furniture, eyes wild as Hannibal Lecter's.
I'd never read enough to get ahead at dinner party conversations,
destined for a man who wouldn't dance, play Scrabble, or entertain
the friends I brought home for him to love.

CONNECTION TO RECOVERY

 I can look at my list and see where I actually had a choice,
or have a choice now. I may not have been able to change
facts, but I can change the judgment I made about myself
based on those facts. I can let my Inner Loving Parent tell
my Inner Child: "I know you felt powerless as a child, but I
will help you find your power now. We can talk about it and
make healthy choices." I can see how far I have come in
recovery from the wounds of my childhood.

Confusing Love and Pity.

The man I later married had been a combat veteran who lost a good deal of his hearing in battle in Vietnam. This triggered my desire to help him:

> *I'd Never Met a Vet*
>
> *Blond and boyish, charcoal*
> *suited, looking for the answers in*
> *law books at our summer job. He didn't*
> *talk about it, but somehow everybody knew –*
> *he'd fought as a Marine in Vietnam.*
>
> *I pursued his pain relentlessly, until from sheer*
> *exhaustion, I suppose, he married me. Over time,*
> *scenes emerged like bursts of pressure cooker steam:*

A nineteen year old Marine, frantic minutes of the death watch;

delivering a baby under fire, splashing vodka as a disinfectant,
an Asian woman babbling words he couldn't grasp.

How can I divorce myself from war, when
I can see the other shore, where circles rippled
by the stones enlarge, then flatten to a sober sheen?

CONNECTION TO RECOVERY

Today I realize that I was attracted to the drama my husband represented. He seemed like a bird with a broken wing, and I was just the one to fix him! I can be gentle with myself and remind myself that I did not make a mistake. It was inevitable that I would find another Adult Child to love.

PROMPT:

1. Write about anyone you have been drawn to because you felt sorry for them. Write about what happened.

2. Write a list poem of all the ways you might try to help or rescue that person. Be outrageous if you wish. I might write about inviting the president to come for dinner and give my husband a silver star. Or treating him like the tin woodman in Dorothy and the Wizard of Oz by giving him a heart. Be playful. It's a good antidote to how serious we get in our efforts to rescue.

Shortly after we started dating in 1976, my mother was coming to New York to have dinner with me. I invited him to join us and he accepted. Then he stood us up. He had no real excuse. "I had to work" is what he said. When someone makes commitments and doesn't show up, it's a sign to walk away. I refused to speak to him for two years, even when our offices were side-by-side. When he finally apologized, we began to date again. He never met my mother. By then she was dead of cancer. I told myself he'd just been afraid of commitment. I told myself he needed me, that I could "help" him.

Yet I know he is an Adult Child too. My husband grew up with a cold, demanding father who had been born in Moscow. His family fled in the Russian revolution. His father arrived in the U.S. knowing no English, learned the language, graduated from the Bronx High School of Science, went to law school, became an intelligence officer in World War II and married his professor's daughter. He reminded my husband that he didn't measure up. The Professor read the paper, all of it. Every day. In this poem, my husband adopts some of the same behaviors as his father:

> *The Dailies*
>
> *You read the papers daily, cover to cover,*
> *as your father did, absorbing, then regurgitating,*
> *facts: weather, brutalities inflicted by one deluded*
> *nation on another, discoveries, awards,*
>
> *as if the answer lies in neatly folded pages, as if*
> *the ink that sinks into your pores will mark you*
> *as a man who knows the score,*
>
> *as if there's something you have yet to learn*
> *that will resolve some nagging shame, some question*
> *about justice in an indifferent universe.*
>
> *I want to punch though the New York Times*
> *you hide behind, prove there is no secret you*
> *have yet to learn, that facts won't yield the peace*
> *you're longing for,*

remind you that your dad, long-dead, can no longer grill you
at the dinner table, smile his satisfaction when you
can't recall the name of England's third Prime Minister.

It's not that I don't care about the news.
It's just that I know all I need to know –
I can't fix anyone or anything,

except what circles in this sunlit living room,
you, behind the morning paper, me, unwilling
to interrupt you, take your hand and lead you

to the patch of grass out back,
show you where the first violets of spring
have just sprung up.

CONNECTION TO RECOVERY

This poem surprised me by a "turn" at the end, a change in direction that surprises the reader (and sometimes the writer!) I know how to help my husband and myself. What do I gain by refusing to take his hand? Why do I insist he be the first one to reach for me? Often, I am simply afraid of being rejected. My poetry can often show me the path of kindness and compassion, even as I am stamping my feet and acting like my inner two-year-old.

PROMPT:

1. Write about a person in your life who is an alcoholic or Adult Child. Put the two of you together in the poem and see what each would say to the other.
2. Write about your partner's pain and confusion in trying to please parents who couldn't be pleased. Make up an incident if you don't know one.

Attraction to Dysfunctional People

Many of us in recovery are baffled as to how we ended up romantically tangled with an alcoholic, workaholic, narcissist, Adult Child, or other dysfunctional person. Didn't we know better? This was a personality we grew up with, a cycle of drama that released adrenalin and made us feel alive. Normal people were "boring." We were programmed from childhood to seek out such people. I can recall my mother criticizing my High School boyfriend as lacking in pizzazz and personality. Today, I see that she was addicted to my father's personality.

Most of my boyfriends in later years fit the pattern of out-sized personalities and dramatic narcissists. Many were Adult Children.

Watching Walter Cronkite

His dad died when he was three. Mine hung on
longer, half-dead from Gallo and despair.
We found each other with the radar
of children unused to being lucky.

Nightly, we'd sit on his college couch, drink
gin, and listen to the man we called "Walt":

"Today, 30 servicemen dead in Vietnam.
Tornados flattened a Midwest mobile park.
Gas prices rose again."

Beneath his newsman's voice, a lyric of authority,
and though we knew he couldn't see us, bathed in cool blue
cathode rays, we straightened up and listened close.

He sat behind a desk. We imagined a dining table.
He wore a suit and tie. We saw a cardigan, worn
at elbows. His desk was clear of papers, pens.

We saw a jello salad jiggling its bits of pineapple
holding out its promise of a tart explosion on the tongue.
As our ice cubes melted, shrank in our mouths,

we were mesmerized as if our horoscope had said
tomorrow would be sunny, our fortunes would improve.
Twenty-two minutes. He signed off: "And that's the way it was."

CONNECTION TO RECOVERY

This boyfriend was odd, even by Berkeley standards. He always wore a black suit and white starched shirt. In that respect, he was clearly dramatic. But he loved me and cared for me in the way I imagine both of us would have liked to have been cared for as children. He died before I could make amends for taking him for granted.

PROMPT:

1. Write about a relationship, past or current, with a dysfunctional person. What did you expect? What did you get?

2. Write about a TV show that made you feel safe as a young person. Explore why that might have been true.

I was attracted to the man I would later marry when we were both young lawyers. We co-hosted a party for new associates at his large apartment in the Village. He went out for a bottle of liquor and returned covered with blood. A bum had tried to take it from him and hadn't counted on confronting an ex-Marine. When I heard the doorbell ring, I found Larry, covered in blood on the step. "Don't tell anyone," he said. "Ok, ok, let's clean you up." Drama. Secrets. I loved it.

Years after Vietnam, my husband still reaches for a handgun, which he calls a sidearm, when he hears a loud noise. His trauma is stored deeply in his body. I know that the first symptom of PTSD is denial, so I'm not surprised that he says he just has a "startle reflex."

I became addicted to the drama of his service in Vietnam. He was angry about the following poem, which won an award, because he felt I had "betrayed him." He didn't want people to know that he would kill a dog to end its suffering. I found his action courageous and compassionate. I thought he would see that I was proud of him. I was amazed that he felt I had portrayed him as cold-hearted when my intent was the opposite. It is clearly a dramatic story.

Sometimes He Comes Home Bloody

with splatters, battered fists, shards of glass
from broken windows embedded in his flesh,
droplets, puddles, smears, stains –

this time he arrives with shirt and tie
askew, splashed with spots of blood.
At first I think he's here at home,

but as he tells me what he's done,
he's back in that God-forsaken jungle.
Tonight, the dog sprang out of nowhere

on the dark highway underpass,
thunked under wheels, then dragged
itself to higher ground, where he found it --

guts exposed, bleeding, beyond a medic's
aid. And he knows what to do, trained with
the eye of triage to tend the ones who can

be stitched, patched, amputated back to life.
Those who can't be saved get triple morphine
or another form of mercy. There is no exercise

for this in basic training, no instructions
on the unthinkable, no discussion about
the worth of one life or another, but

as he squeezes air from limp and matted fur,
he's doing what he's trained to do,
what he's done before, what he'll do again.

CONNECTION TO RECOVERY

This poem reminds me that my husband and I share a story about his years in Vietnam and how they have affected our marriage and my recovery. I share my recovery program with him when appropriate. I don't keep my recovery a secret. I also share my writing about him before I send it into the world. I check my motivations in writing about him: will it help me or others in recovery or is it simply a dramatic story? When I can articulate a higher motivation, I know what is appropriate to publish.

PROMPT:

1.Write about a situation that you and your partner see very differently. See if you can write it from both points of view. Perhaps it works into a dialogue poem. Is there a concrete image or a metaphor than can stand for your disagreement?

2.Write a poem that begins "Sometimes he/she comes home . . . " and fill in the blank. See what happens.

175

The drama of my husband's war service affected me much in the way secondhand smoke affects those in a room who aren't smoking. In the following poem, I ended with an image from an old photograph of my husband. This was not my first ending for the poem, but it showed how my thinking evolved. It moves from the drama to a scene that shows he was an innocent child.

Secondhand Smoke

Home from Vietnam, you said the past was past.
It's back--a GI boot abandoned in the dust,
men crouched in doorways wielding M-16's,

a dead soldier, swinging from high tension wires.
Smoke sifts through your dawn like a thousand fallen
angels, searching for a perch among the wreckage of Iraq.

The New York Times assaults with bloody children, buses
burning. Shell casings form a desolate mosaic on Iraqi streets.
 Avoid the news. It's better for your nerves.

You command our deck alone at 5 a.m.
Peonies salute with crimson blooms. Clutching coffee
and a cigarette, you're lost within a haze of steam and smoke.

I shut the sliding door against the fumes, inhale
the still suburban morning, picture you when you were ten,
posing on a pony on a New York City sidewalk.

CONNECTION TO RECOVERY
I can transform an image of drama to one of serenity by remembering that even people who trigger me were once innocent children, just like me. I can also set boundaries when I recognize "secondhand smoke" is affecting me. I can close the door.

PROMPT:

1.Writing from a standpoint of compassion and kindness, tell a story of your partner that reclaims part of his or her childhood or that extends compassion or gratitude for what he or she has accomplished.

2.Find a photograph (like the one I found of my husband on a pony) and knit it into a poem that is not about that photo. See how describing his/her younger self brings compassion into the poem.

FINDING A HIGHER POWER

Before I began recovery, I worked with a Spiritual Director. The process failed. I was in denial and too defended to make use of what she had to offer. When I told her about a situation, she'd ask, "how does that make you feel?" That question enraged me. I had three words for feelings: happy, mad and sad. I felt mad that she knew some "secret language" that I didn't know. There was some answer I knew she wanted to hear but for the life of me, I had no idea what it was. It was as if she were speaking Latin. It was the language of feelings. This triggered my childhood fear of not knowing the right answer.

The other block to working with a spiritual director was my conception of God. I couldn't get any consistent "picture" in my mind. When she'd ask how I pictured God, all I could see was the Bible School picture of a bearded man on a throne. Then came Jehovah--a judgmental God who planned a cataclysmic war of Armageddon that would kill anyone who wasn't a Jehovah's Witness. A God who would kill millions of good people just because they didn't join a tiny religious sect was a God I rejected. Because a child's vision of God is often modeled on their father, and as my father was mercurial and often violent, I was not able to translate a loving dad to a loving God.

Eventually, I began to see a Higher Power as female—an angel of light in white robes. I was afraid of the cellar in my childhood home. The cellar was evil, dark with a dirt floor and weird crevices made of brick. It smelled moldy and spidery. My director tried to guide me down the steps to the cellar in meditation. I refused for weeks. But when I imagined an angel bathed in light standing on the steps before me, I was willing to let the angel guide me not all the way down, but at least on the steps. Today, I see the "steps" as a reference to the steps of recovery, although it would take many years for me to find the rooms of recovery.

Envisioning a Higher Power

When I began recovery, my sponsor asked me to describe my Higher Power. Once again, I choked. I reverted to the Higher Power of my childhood. She suggested I formulate my own Higher Power. Today, my Higher Power lives inside me. It is the "still, small voice" that reminds me to depend on spiritual principles, such as kindness, compassion, forgiveness, truth, love and hope. To reach this Higher Power, I must break through my own defenses and be gentle with myself. When I can calm myself and listen to the voice within me, I pretty much always know the right thing to do or say.

Today, I believe there is a Higher Power that desires recovery for all of us. When I think of those I love, I connect with the power of love as a universal force. I also experience a Higher Power in the rooms of recovery and in my writing. When I mentally "revisit" places where I have had profound spiritual experiences, I know a Higher Power has been at work. Due to childhood religious abuse, I may never be able to visualize God as an entity with the power to grant prayers of the righteous or punish sinners. Fortunately, we in recovery can find a Higher Power that works for us. In this section, I offer many avenues to experience a Higher Power. Take what works for you.

In the following poem, I thought about my husband's nightmares from Vietnam and my hope that he can someday stop blaming God for the horrific death and destruction he experienced. I believe God comes creeping into dreams, giving signs and warnings that I may not be consciously aware of.

Night's Blessing

When the night sounds blend together
the rhythmic click of the cicadas,
frogs' forlorn love song,
the wheels of trucks on a distant highway.

When the dark becomes a different kind
of day, revealing shapes in shadows,
when the only sound's a sigh,
a stretch, a quick intake of breath.

When you mumble in a nightmare:
Don't send me over there,
bolt awake at 5am, slip downstairs,
take up your vigil waiting for a hint of pink,

That's when God comes creeping in,
hiding in the undergrowth of half truth,
waiting to be discovered in the slow
advance of dawn, its widening complexion.

CONNECTION TO RECOVERY

When I stop intellectualizing about God and feel a source of goodness within me, I can access a Higher Power. I can be gentle with myself and allow a Higher Power to show up in unexpected places. I can recognize that my fight with God is from my childhood and accept it does not affect my life today.

PROMPT:

1. Envision a Higher Power in your life and turn it into an object. Where is it hiding? What would you need to do to find it?

2. Ask your inner child to describe their Higher Power. Use your non-dominant hand. Read what your inner child wrote and write a poem describing how that makes you feel.

3. Imagine how a benevolent Higher Power would view a lost person. Write a poem from that benevolent perspective to yourself.

Often, objects of inspiration and comfort from childhood can help me connect with a Higher Power, as in the poem below.

> *Comforter*
>
> *An eiderdown, soft, lightweight, hovers*
> *over shifting rustle of limbs and feet*
> *as they settle into sleep*
>
> *The first snowbells of spring, violets clutched*
> *in grubby fingers, a gift for mother offered*
> *in a silver vase shaped like a Grecian urn*
>
> *A voice that needs no fanfare, proclamation, adoration,*
> *a truth that settles like a flock of geese*
> *on a moonlit lake beneath a summer sky*
>
> *The first two-wheeler, school bus ride,*
> *night away from home, the tryouts for the team,*
> *an expanse of tomorrows when you can try again*
>
> *A tune, a phrase, a puppy's kiss,*
> *Van Gogh, Michelangelo, the gossamer*
> *of a dragonfly, the taste of ripe tomatoes*

the touch of silk, satin binding on a blanket,
strands of baby hair, an old dog's brittle
coat, perfection woven into a lullaby

CONNECTION TO RECOVERY

I love to nap under a white plush blanket. I feel protected and safe. Finding images like that help me connect to a Higher Power.

PROMPT:

1. Visualize the qualities of unconditional love and write a poem in which you list objects or beings that embody that feeling for you.

2. What brings you safety? Write about that as a Higher Power.

Animals as a Spiritual Experience

I could never risk eye contact with my father when he was drunk. Even if he was looking at me, I didn't trust that he truly saw me. His pale blue eyes when drunk were demonic. By contrast, dogs cement relationships with humans through eye contact. I can look to pets when searching for the feeling of being unconditionally loved. I wrote this poem in my dog's voice.

Eye Contact

She wants me to look at her.
This is so perplexing.
What can she gain by gazing in my eyes?

Sometimes she takes my head
in both her hands, swerves it to her,
and waits. I don't know what we're waiting for.

She doesn't know I've been up since six,
skittered downstairs when he woke,
doesn't know I've been fed, let out to poop,
that we've been busy pondering the New York Times.

But something pulls me back upstairs.
I love the curled round soft of her,
her sleepy smell, last night's Chanel.
I love it that she doesn't wash her face.
I don't wash mine either.

She sees me, pulls me to her, pleased
because she thinks I'm pleased.

Even though I'm alone, now that the mutt
and poodle left, I don't miss them.
But I miss her. Each time she drives off,
I think "maybe I should spend more time
practicing my eye contact."

My dog literally jumps up and down when I reach for my running shoes. She is always happy when I come in the door, even if I have left her for hours. In one terrible romantic breakup, I recall cuddling with a kitty for comfort and love. I am reminded of how my dad loved animals. Even an alcoholic can find unconditional love with an animal.

PROMPT:

1.Write about a childhood pet and the role it played in your life as a metaphor for something missing in your life. Was it a source of unconditional love for you? What happened?

2.If you didn't have a pet, write about a stuffed animal or other object that brought you unconditional love as a child.

Music Can Invite a Higher Power

Music can bypass my thinking mind and resonate with a deeper part of me. When I recorded affirmations that I wanted to hear from my parents, I played soft meditation music in the background. Music both soothes and elevates. There are a few songs that create a longing for connection and a feeling that there is a Higher Power greater than I am. Some I heard in church as an adult. One hymn's lyrics said, "Is it I Lord? I have heard you calling in the night. I will go, Lord, where you lead me, I will hold your people in my heart." I cried every time we sang it. I knew I was being called to something and I knew it was bigger than my family. I just didn't know what. When I toured the Mormon Tabernacle, the choir was rehearsing. When they sang: " God be with you til we meet again," tears flooded my eyes.

I respond the same way to certain secular songs. When I hear "I had the time of my life . . . and I owe it all t0 you," by Bill Medley, I recall ordering a singing telegram of the song for my daughter's 17th birthday at school. "Unchained Melody" by the Righteous Brothers has the same effect. "I've hungered for your touch a long lonely time." It's easy to hear romance in these songs, which transports me to my teenaged years. But I can also hear a fundamental longing for a connection with a power greater than myself.

I Owe it All to You

I've hungered for your touch
I will go where you lead me
Til we meet again
I will hold you in my heart

The time of my life
I heard you calling in the night
For a long lonely time
with you til we meet again

I've had the time of my life
holding in my heart
where you lead me
And I owe it all to you

CONNECTION TO RECOVERY

I can let music, particularly songs I've loved for years, speak to my longing to connect with a Higher Power. I can see words or phrases I thought applied to romance remind me that the love from my Higher Power is a powerful romance.

Children as a Spiritual Experience

When my eldest daughter was born and wheeled into my room, I was astonished: her tiny face was God! I need a God with a face on it—and not the face of an old mean guy. Of course, as time went on, my daughter became an ordinary child, but I recall how blessed I felt to become a mother and how her face shone. Now that I know I have an inner Higher Power that incorporates the spiritual values others ascribe to a deity – love, compassion, forgiveness, patience— it no longer surprises me that I actually "saw" God as something that until moments before had quite literally been a part of me.

I return to my love for children when I feel myself losing touch with the God within. I remember that even when my own girls ignored me, called me names, and got mad at me, I still loved them. My biggest fear when I was expecting my second child—that I wouldn't have enough love to go around--dissipated magically when I discovered my quota of love doubled when she was born. This was quite literally a miracle, one that is available every day to every parent. My instinct in knitting a sweater for my darling daughter is the same instinct I wish a Higher Power to bestow on me.

186

Swans and Hearts

My daughter asked for a sweater when she turned five.
She wanted swans and hearts. I, mother of the quick fix,

the good enough, always sure the inside wouldn't show,
was stumped. Swans and hearts would take some planning.

I found my mother's needles in her knitting bag, faded stripes
of silk with narrow pockets sewn inside.

Did I have it in me, the knowledge of the fingers, which way
to wrap the yarn, how to transfer stitches, cast on, cast off?

They say it's based on instinct, like mothering.
I feared I had the instincts of a coat rack.

I picked bright pink, with white swans on a turquoise sea,
coaxed out a pattern, calculated colors, knit one row at

a time. The swans and hearts began to grow, separated
on the right side, but underneath, linked by strands of pink.

CONNECTION TO RECOVERY

Knitting and yarn are metaphors for family
connection. I see in this poem that I have adopted
two of my mother's loving qualities—her love for
children and her ability to knit—and bestowed them
on my own daughters. This reminds me of both my
connection to my Higher Power and the type of love
that I have known as a child and that is available to
me as an adult.

PROMPT:

1.Find an object that demonstrates your love for another and write about it. In this poem it was the sweater I wasn't sure I could make.

2.In this poem, my being able to knit a sweater challenged my belief about my ability. What secret project have you been able to accomplish that you didn't think you could do? Did love play a part in it?

3.Write about how it feels to be around children who let themselves play and have fun. What feelings and memories do they evoke in you?

4. The strands of pink yarn beneath the sweater are a metaphor for the invisible strands that bind us to our children. Write about what invisible connections bind you to those you love and to your Higher Power.

The following poem is based on a photograph of my daughters during rose season in our local park. Even when I didn't see their personalities as clearly as I do now, they were already apparent. And if today they squabble or complain about each other, they are joined together by love. The poem imagines that pain will enter the picture at some point, as in fact it did. But I can return to a spot where there was calm, beauty and grace. That metaphorical "place" is accessible to me any time I choose to focus on it.

Portrait in Elizabeth Park

Posed in the gazebo for their photograph,
my three girls are framed by roses,
hot pink, deep red, pale yellow, their
first unfurling, the scent of innocence

on the brink of overwhelming. Eleanor
and Susan perch on a wooden bench. Eleanor,
the eldest, hovers, ready to rein in the sprawl
of Susan, a five-year-old who hasn't learned

to pose her legs together. My middle daughter,
Claire, has wandered, sits off on the grass, peers
into tight petals of a bud, as if she could foretell
rapture or rejection from its folds.

I'd dressed them in flowered chintz, hoping
they would complement the garden's bright explosion,
after months of steady rain and gray days,
which seemed required to make me grateful

for a garden planted purely for delight.
By mid-July, I know the roses will have dried
and dulled, the thorns turned brittle,
another season looming in the shadow.

But for today, they are as perfect as
new blooms, a corsage pinned on for a prom,
hope and spring imprinted on my mind.

I can use this image in my meditation. The wilting flowers at the end remind me not to romanticize my years of motherhood. The fact that my girls' personalities were so clearly already established makes me laugh and also lightens my sense of responsibility for their adult lives. It reminds me not to take myself so seriously.

PROMPT:

1.Write about a "place" can you recall or imagine where love was palpably present. If there isn't such a place, make one up. You can put your parents there, children (even if you don't have any). Make the place as specific as the rose garden. Don't try to avoid the direction the poem wants to take. Let it take you there.

2.Imagine that characteristics of a loved one, such as my eldest trying to control the youngest, are endearing rather than annoying. How would you talk about them?

3.Imagine the sense of comfort and ease that you longed for as a child. Give that sense an object or a place. Write about how you felt. You may want to begin with something in your life today and see if you can connect it back to some person or event from childhood.

4.Find a photo of yourself as a child. Find the spiritual in you and write about it.

Another of my happy memories was lying in my bed in the morning and hearing my little girls babble in their cribs. They sounded so happy and full of life. Even though I couldn't understand a word, I imbued their babble the same way I do birdsong: as a hymn to the wonder and beauty of life. That sound was the secret language of a Higher Power.

Morning Song

My bed is a warm nest, sun spilling in the northern window,
a streak of red and yellow leaves almost at the height

of saturation before becoming brittle, turning brown.
I burrow down. The birds are chirping cheerily.

I soften my hearing, tune out discord, imagine it's
one happy family singing a campfire song.

Then across the hall, my baby wakes. I hear her rustle,
then a babble so glorious, as light as lemon meringue,

airy with radiance. I want to find a tape recorder to
capture it for winter mornings after she finds words,

fearful I'll forget the magic of sounds I can't transcribe,
a hymn to all creation, the miracle of morning, a chord

that shimmers from her room to mine, invisible, electric,
as if a thousand songbirds perched along the line.

I think of my Higher Power as the babble of my infants. I don't need to understand the words, just the feeling. This reminds me that there are sounds all around me that I "tune out" daily. By training my ears to listen for birds, airplanes, the dog snoring at my feet, I connect into the real world. I become totally present.

PROMPT:

1.Explore feelings of comfort and being connected to the spirit by working with the five senses to evoke the feeling. In the poem above, I use the sound of a baby's babble. You can find sounds in nature, the touch of a kiss, an eyelash, the taste of something memorable and let it guide you to the spirit.

2.Explore the sense of trust and tenderness you or your inner child felt around certain people who embodied kindness or other admirable qualities.

Nature as a Spiritual Experience

For many of us, a Higher Power reveals itself in nature. Perhaps this is because nature is often a meditative place, one where we disconnect from our compulsions and obsessions. But nature can also be a place that shocks us to the core. This following poem addresses a time when I was sure a Higher Power was showing itself through the sun.

Revelation

One Sunday afternoon in January
driving west on Fern,
I saw a red sun so otherworldly,
looming gigantic in the sky,
the street, my life,
that I was sure:
"This is it."
The Apocalypse.
It will be fire after all.

Yet cars passed by, no one braking,
no one throwing open doors,
no one on his knees,
no one calling "Mother."
No conflagration.
Not even smoke.

My car radio continued playing Mozart.
No "Wah Wah" early warning system.
No sirens, fire trucks or ambulance.
Silence on a Sunday afternoon.

Alone in my astonishment, I had no one
to tell, no one to pull over, no arm to grab,
to point as Lucifer and his minions
hurtled overhead.

Then the sun began to move,
inched toward the sea,
although I couldn't see a sea.
A prophet without proof.

CONNECTION TO RECOVERY

I was shocked. It must have been only seconds before I realized the blood-red sun was a natural phenomenon, but it reminds me that nature can present some amazing sights. Sometimes, high drama is required to get my attention. I was forced to pay attention, to be grateful my natural phenomenon was not an earthquake, tsunami, or forest fire.

PROMPT:

1.Write about any experience in nature where you felt close to a Higher Power or where you were shocked out of your normal consciousness.

2.Write about the power of nature and your powerlessness over nature. You can write about a flood, earthquake or other natural disaster. What does this reveal about your connection to a Higher Power?

3.Ask a scene in nature to reveal something to you about its power in your life.

I use trees as a metaphor for the Higher Power of my community in recovery. They quite literally "hold me up," often in ways I don't see. I use this metaphor in a poem I wrote about a time when my middle child developed an eating disorder.

Valley of Shadows

The winding road descends from sun-struck hills
to reach Muir Woods, where redwoods rise
three hundred feet enveloped in thick fog.

Dwarfed by massive trunks of battered bark,
my daughter's legs in shorts stick out like twigs.
She thinks she'll be perfect if she starves herself.

These trees survive the summer's drought
on filigrees of fog that drift in from the sea,
catch on their needles, condense,

and fall to the forest floor. They grow in circles,
shelter shoots that sprout from trunks.
Their roots entwine with those nearby

to hold each other up. She is beyond
the reach of roots, the comfort of the scent
of loam, of sea spray, new growth, and decay.

Yet when I reach down with my hand,
she takes it as she did when she was six,
when I knew all the ways to keep her safe.

The image of the trees holding themselves up, with their roots in a circle, reminds me that in recovery I am not alone and that I have others to help hold me up. It also reminds me that I need to be those roots for other people in recovery, working slowly, sometimes unseen, in order to help hold them up.

PROMPT:

1.Write about the life force of nature and its resilience. How do you connect to that power?

2.Imagine that an object in nature is a source of wisdom and comfort for you. Let it speak to you.

Places Where You Had a Spiritual Experience

Sometimes we have a spiritual experience we don't recognize because it doesn't look the way we expect it to. If I am looking for a burning bush accompanied by the voice of God, I've limited the definition of a spiritual experience. Perhaps I need to define it first. If sin, as some say, is any practice or thought pattern that separates me from God, then a spiritual experience would be any practice or thought pattern that connects me with God.

If it is too difficult to envision a spiritual experience, I can look for instances where the "fruits" of the spirit appear. Saint Francis articulated them beautifully centuries ago in his famous prayer, which urges us to take the attention off ourselves and put it on others. Here are the tools he suggested: love, forgiveness, harmony, faith, hope, light, joy, comfort, understanding. Now, I may not want to act using these tools of the spirit, I may get selfish and resist, but I absolutely know what they are. I have no doubt how to use the hammer of comfort or the screwdriver of forgiveness.

I had a sponsor who suggested that I list the places where I had had a spiritual experience and "visit there regularly." Initially, I got caught in the burning bush scene—where, I wondered, had God been speaking, even if I defined God as a voice within me? I have found that if I ask and keep asking, the moments will appear. They lend themselves beautifully to a "list poem."

Here and There

My hospital room, my first baby wheeled in, her tiny baby face aglow with mystery—the mystery of me and not me, who she will become, and I think, God, yes. There you are.

The Mormon Tabernacle Choir, a man, the single black face in a sea of white, singing: God Be With You Til We Meet Again. And I think: God.

The window with organdy curtains, outside white fences, horses grazing. The grandfather clock ticks, ticks, chimes. I long for that clock like our puppy, her first night bundled at our hearth, nestled with a clock, to remind her of her mother.

The doctor's scale that said my anorexic daughter had gained 10 pounds in a month, impossible. My daughter, returned to the living,

197

her desperation to be thin outweighed by the demands of marijuana. Thank God for marijuana.

At my tenth wedding anniversary, my husband whole-heartedly recited vows before a God he privately called a maggot. For me. For our two daughters. For the third, who unbeknownst to us was even then, stirring.

The hymn in church, "Is it I Lord, I have heard you calling in the night. I will go Lord, where you lead me. I will hold your people in my heart." I don't know yet who these people will be. The call a mystery. I'll find it years later in a church basement.

Fern Brook, the perfect peace of a perfect summer afternoon, children chirping among smooth stones, the minnows, the waving leaves. Everybody flowing in the same direction.

A sleeping granddaughter, nestled near my neck, breathing in her baby smell, of soap and milk and skin, her tiny fingers grasping one of mine.

My dog Belle, never more than ten feet from my feet. Dozing, waiting, leaping at the jangle of the leash. Always at the door when I return. Yes. There you are.

The first violets of spring when I am eight. I reach down each tender stem and pinch, gather in a silver urn, a surprise for mother. Each year. A surprise.

The Madonna of Justice, a painting with Mary and a giant book, a Latin inscription. She calls to me. Mystery. Law. Rules. Books. Babies. Angels. She wants my help. She wants to help me.

Three kittens, all black, using me as a playscape on a sick day, the delight of kitten fur, pink tongues. Suddenly, they tire, drop, sleep. And I think: Yes. This is what you feel like.

CONNECTION TO RECOVERY

I must write down the places where I feel the spirit or I risk forgetting them or robbing them of their power. My disease wants me to "forget." I see that some of my spiritual experiences felt powerful at the time, such as seeing the painting called "The Madonna of Justice." Others, such as the afternoon at Fern Brook in the poem below called "Visible," were ordinary, but I recall feeling an overwhelming sense of peace. I can often find spiritual experiences by looking for odd "coincidences."

PROMPT:

1. List the places where you had a spiritual experience and "visit" one of them in a poem.

2. Sit quietly and think of situations or places that seemed at the time a mystery, or an epiphany, or an unusual connection with a person, place or thing. Think of moments that brought you to tears or to laughter. Try not to judge them. Make a list of these situations.

3. See if any of your incidents "connect." Rearrange your poem to bring them closer together.

4. To add energy to your poem, you can write both where you found the experience and where you did not. This is called working with "contraries."

Frequently, in meditation, people are "guided" to imagine a beach or a mountain as a place of serenity. These are good ideas and may work for you. I find that those places have too much emotional baggage for me. They are places where I am "supposed to" feel a certain way. As an Adult Child, I resist authority, even if it's a meditation leader. As I thought about it, I realized my "place" was much closer to home.

Visible

Beneath the brook that swirls in from the upper bend,
then tumbles out of sight beneath a footbridge, stones sparkle

like gray pearls. I know they'll fade to ordinary plucked out
and placed on a windowsill. Their magic needs restraint.

Minnows zig zag in their glitziness, brown punctuation marks,
commas that say to breathe or hold a thought. Yet they seem

bent on some odd mission, something requiring quick response
and unity, a mystery to me.

Beneath the water, my daughters dip their fingers, stir it up,
content with just each other and with me, a rarity.

The silt swirls. They watch it sift downwards. The minnows
are still milling, unconcerned, unmystified.

The leaves form a patchwork canopy that casts a moving shadow,
the grass nearby as soft as prayer.

My children chatter, laughter and surprise as they try to touch
the fish, splash each other, decode the language of the brook.

Beneath my thoughts of dinner, homework done, not done,
my struggle to control their juggle for position on our family tree,

a language, eerie as a keekowah, bubbles up, notes of shifting leaves,
the water's gloss, bird calls, the minnows with their minnow music.

Beneath all this, a moment born of happenstance, when mystery
turns palpable, becomes a silken cord that links us to the water,
trees, birds, even to the minnows, that marks this place, this grace.

CONNECTION TO RECOVERY

This poem reminds me that my best entry point into retrieving memory is to concentrate on feelings. Where have I felt complete, peaceful, safe, at one with my surroundings? Once I access the feelings, the memories will often come. The return of feelings is one hallmark that recovery has begun.

PROMPT:

1.Write about any place where you felt totally at peace, whole and complete.

2.If you have trouble finding such a place, make one up. Ask yourself where have you been when you felt fulfilled and flourishing? This may lead to an experience that you only now see as having been spiritual.

Being "Good Enough"

As an Adult Child, I seek praise and fear criticism. As a mother, I wanted to be the best. In recovery, we give up our desire to be perfect and learn humility and being right-sized. In the following poem, I recall young mothers being interchangeable at the pool. This is a comforting memory for me, because it reminds me I'm not so special. (Although for the little kid reaching for a mom's leg, I'm good enough!)

The Wading Pool

It's gone, that ten-inch pool surrounded by chain link
at Fern Park, where toddlers clustered, lurched,
and spluttered, grabbed hold of their mom,
or any other mother, which is what I truly loved,

knowing I was good enough, they, in their diaper-puffy
bathing suits, ungainly pink ruffled bottoms, like exotic birds
that balance weight on reed-thin legs, a mystery
of physics. They'd clutch my shin for ballast, balance me.

That was back when all us moms were interchangeable,
likewise all the kids, when every child was talented and smart,
all headed for the Gifted Program, when we all smacked our lips
on chicken nuggets, found prizes in our Happy Meals.

Our kids like plastic sparkle ponies waited at the starting gate.
Bring back the wading pool, I want to tell the Council.
Bring back those summer afternoons, when we'd head home
for naptime, chloriney and content.

Many of my happiest memories are from "ordinary" days. When I accept myself as not needing to be "superior," I integrate my Character Trait of super-responsibility and being controlling and become my True Self.

PROMPT:

1.Write about any situation where you were "good enough," where you were able to accept not being the best. Looking back, recall the cakes you baked that fell apart, the car you drove that wasn't the newest model, the report you wrote that you struggled to get right and then wasn't read. Allow yourself to be ordinary.

2.Think about a childhood situation where you believed you weren't good enough. See if you can find something today you appreciate about your younger self in that situation. Find something that reveals you weren't what you believed at the time.

Prayer and Meditation

Connecting with a Higher Power through prayer is particularly difficult for me as an Adult Child. First, I am defiant of authority, which makes "God" problematic. Next, many of us have trust issues from childhood. Often there was no one to help us. Why should anyone help us now? We lacked healthy models of unconditional love and guidance. Finally, we are driven to keep busy, and prayer often requires us to slow down.

I can start by sitting down with nothing to do. On my front porch, I have two Adirondack chairs. I imagine I am on an ocean-going vessel, with a seemingly endless vista.

Meditation From my Front Step

The water is the indigo
of my mother's eyes.
Sunlight shivers at the horizon,
so fierce a line, I can believe
the world is flat.

The ship rocks, hums its
heartbeat, nestled in a blanket
of unfolding waves. The whitecaps
of the ego; the surge of id below.

Welcome, welcome to the breeze,
the call of gulls so far from shore,
insistent in their hunger and the hunt.
I wonder where they sleep and when.

I'm floating, emptying my mind
of ports of call, visas, checkpoints,
souvenirs, the clamor of tomorrow.

I think of tea at 4pm, then realize
it's only ten. No need to wonder,
worry, will there be scones again,
blueberry jam, cream or honey.
Will there be a place for me
at the captain's table?

Practice. Practice patience.
The ship will go no faster
if I plan ahead.
I was here yesterday.
I'll be back tomorrow.
Rocking. humming, Floating.
On my way. Or not.

You can see that the fear of not having a place at the "captain's table" snuck into my poem. The "captain" stands for my Higher Power. I'm afraid of being left out. I need to remind myself that tea isn't until 4 pm and it's only 10 am. I can take a breath and trust that there will be a place for me.

PROMPT:

1.Write about a place where you could simply sit and be at peace. Who or what would be there? How would you calm your thoughts or accept them?

2.Use sensory description. What does the place sound like? Is the sun shining? What can you smell? What sensations do you feel in your body? Be as specific as you can.

I can also connect with a Higher Power by writing about the gifts of the spirit that I hope to gain in recovery. By reminding myself that these gifts are freely available to me, I can see a Higher Power working in my life.

Why Am I Here?

To receive a blessing, like Jacob wrestling with the angel.
a blessing for my elder years, these years of letting go.

To receive the wisdom of the teachers, those teachers
that I didn't recognize, hiding in the corner, silent,
the ones who didn't seem to have too much to say.

To let go of my ideas of how it should be done.
To let it go exactly the way it will unfold.

To remember those who came before.
To honor those before me, to accept their gifts.

To find my deepest self, the self that gives
the perfect fried egg to her child and takes
the broken one herself.

To give the power of writing full rein,
let it take off through the meadow, trust
I won't fall off or be thrown.

To let my writing be an offering to me,
then to see if it is wanted, needed, and offer
freely to those in need.

To create from plenty. To put down praise,
knowing there will never be enough, a sip of praise
setting off a thirst that leads me to the addict's
sick romance.

To believe: there's nowhere else I need to be.
There's nothing else I need to be doing.

CONNECTION TO RECOVERY

Prayer and Meditation are specifically addressed in Step 11. By writing a prayer that questions how I am to behave in the world, I avoid asking for specific things and focus on service and recovery. Part of my prayer is to be my True Self in writing and helping others with their writing and to remember that praise is not my goal. Community and healing are my goals

1.Write a list of all the spiritual tools and awareness that you want from your Higher Power.

2.Notice what you want from your Higher Power is both inspiration to share your gifts and relief from your Character Traits. Try to put both in your prayer.

I can easily get confused by the phrase "God's will." As an Adult Child, whenever an adult tried to get me to do something, I often felt their anger and criticism. And as I am addicted to busy-ness and big-shotism, I thought at first that God's will must involve something dramatic like going to India to solve world hunger. The issue was clarified for me by a friend who said that she believed God's will was that we use our spiritual gifts for the good of ourselves and those around us. This removed some resistance. But not all, as you will see from the poem below:

Take It

Take my will and my life.
No. Not my life.
Let me live until the baby comes,
until I hitch her
on my hip,
until the spit-up
on my shoulder crusts
to dust. Let me have
what you denied my mother.
No. Not my life.

OK. Take my will.
No. Not if it means
I don't get it my way.
That would be in all things—

207

from my wardrobe
to who gets to join
my Book Group,
what I eat,
No. Not if it means
rice and beans
six times a week.

OK. Take my pen.
Take the ink.
Flow it to your will.
Take it. But guarantee
it's blue.
Also let me pick the topic.

OK. Not the pen.
How about the pencil?
It's tight-packed stream
of lead, its shavings
twisted in the sharpener.
Take my sharp-pointed
pencil. Let it scratch
the page, like a divining rod,
bend when it hits water,
essential element,
practicing the loopy Os
of the Palmer Method,
from first grade, hovering
between the sturdy lines
to corral meandering.

Let it scribble past
the cheerful signposts
called Middle School,
graduation, the M.F.A.,
publication, the Pulitzer.
OK. Maybe not the Pulitzer.

Let my pencil, trusty No. 2,
as yellow as a school bus,
let it be the one thing
I surrender.
Let it go where you
would have it go.
But please,
leave me the eraser.

CONNECTION TO RECOVERY

I watch myself give up my will and take it back. This reminds me that this is one of my Adult Child traits. But I write about it lightly, with humor. I can practice not being too serious. I can imagine my Inner Loving Parent's words: "You are perfect just the way you are. I love your writing. I love your joke about the eraser, and the Pulitzer. You are so funny!"

PROMPT:

1.Write about your most outlandish wish for fame and fortune and then imagine giving it away. See what happens.

2.Write a list of a time when you asserted your self will to "make" something happen and it backfired. Imagine if you had used the spiritual tools of compassion, love, forgiveness, and trust instead.

3.Talk back to some accomplishment you achieved and ask it what it would say to you now.

The following poem imagines a monk who thinks he knows God's will for him. He is sure about his "job." Then he becomes less sure:

Monk, Mountainside, Meditation

The early morning birds a call to prayer.
Meditation accomplished through a task.

> Take my hands, Lord
> use them for your work

Reeds collected from the swamplands
weeds dried to yellow husks that smell of musk

> I wet them, try to bend them
> to my will.

How many baskets, Lord?
Ten, then twenty. Fifty-five.

> I have nothing to put in them. No food or water.
> Only questions.

They pile into a jumble on the floor.

Should I hang them
on the wall?

Like stones that circle in a labyrinth,
they form a straw mosaic

> How can I tread this path?
> Where is the holy?

Days, seasons pass. My mind remains a jumble,
filled with fretful, gnawing thoughts.

> Enough? not enough?
> How will I know?

The center shifts, sun slicing through gaps,
I see a crowded wall, lined like an old man's face.

Give me my portion, lord.
Sufficient to this day.

Now I see. I take down every one.
Unravel them. Begin again.

CONNECTION TO RECOVERY

Recovery is a journey, not a destination. That slogan is trite, but true. I will never be "done." But I believe God's will does not involve projects or accomplishments, however worthy the object. For me, God's will is that I use my gifts and talents to benefit others and that I turn my thoughts and acts over to spiritual principles such as kindness and tolerance. Of course I need to "wash, rinse, repeat."

1.Think of a project that you accomplished in life. It may be something you made, something you wrote, a speech, a dog you trained, something that you felt was important and earned you praise. Then imagine it was destroyed or the people you thought were going to praise you did not. Write about it. Use the metaphor of the monk unraveling baskets to find your own metaphor.

2.Write about a time you thought you knew God's will but had a specific outcome in mind. How might the actual outcome have benefited you more than the one you had in mind?

3.Write about a time God's will surprised you or sneaked up on you. For instance, perhaps you moved to be closer to family only to have the family move away. In their flight you hit a bottom and encountered ACA. Without that move you likely wouldn't have found the program.

MAKING AMENDS

Forgiveness, both of ourselves and others, is an important step in recovery. It goes far beyond making amends for our bad behavior. It means changing our behavior and recognizing that things we have done cannot be changed. The consequences of my behavior when I was a college student could have been devastating. I had left the Jehovah's Witnesses and moved in with a boyfriend. This violated the Jehovah's Witness prohibition of pre-marital sex and therefore created a rift between me and my mother, who was still a Jehovah's Witness. We avoided the subject. Had I acknowledged my sexual activity, she would have been obliged to report me to the Witnesses, who would have "dis-fellowshipped me." My mother would be required to shun me. I was living on the west coast and she was in New Jersey. In the following poem, I symbolize my mother's love for me by a yellow shirt she sent to me when I was in college. Her gift told me what she couldn't say:

Happy Spring

Spring comes to Berkeley.
dampness starts to dry.
We march, protest authority.

Brown box from home,
shirt of yellow silk,
drenched in daffodils.

"Happy Spring," the only note,
my mother's olive branch
sunshine wrapped in tissue

"Happy Spring," although
I've broken rules
rejected God's true church.

Found lying with a lover,
I'd be cast out by elders,
my sentence, silence.

"Happy Spring," she dares,
soft silk embrace
She speaks in gifts.

CONNECTION TO RECOVERY

I have been forgiven over and over in my life. It's important to connect with the grace that others have given to me, which helps right-size my judgmental side. I can't begin to make amends to others until I recognize how many people have already forgiven me.

PROMPT:

1. Write about a real or imagined gift from one of your parents or caretakers that tells you that you are loved.

2. Write about a gift you might give to someone in your life today to express forgiveness.

Writing About Forgiveness

How do we know if an amends is sincere? Some of us have said "I'm sorry" over and over without changing our behavior or taking full responsibility. The following poem explores saying "I'm sorry," but blaming someone or something else for our behavior. The poem is based on a famous poem written by William Carlos Williams called "This Is Just To Say." In the poem, the narrator apologizes to someone for eating plums that he knew she was saving for lunch. His apology rings false because in essence he says "the plums were so good, they made me eat them." Many writers have used this form for a fun take-off on an apology that is not really an apology.

Sorry/Not Sorry
       after William Carlos Williams

This is just to say
I have drunk the Chardonnay
that I found in the cabinet, and
which you were probably
saving for dinner.

Forgive me. It washed down
steak and eggs with a satisfying
swig, the crisp aftertaste marrying
so beautifully with the meaty
mastication of the beef.

And besides, the bottle had been there
for weeks, so I knew you could not have
needed it the way I did, could not have
heard it calling, like an exotic bird hidden
in tall trees in the Amazon, harkening
its sacred call, setting off a craving
to capture it, to know the sweet
success of conquering something that
sings a bright new tune.

CONNECTION TO RECOVERY
Are my amends sincere? Am I blaming someone or something else for my behavior? What's the cost to me and them when I do that? I can avoid taking responsibility for my actions by using humor, as this poem does. My humor can be sarcastic, passive-aggressive, or cynical. I can work on using plain "funny" humor that is not at someone else's expense as I become my True Self.

Amends to Ourselves

It's often said in program that we should begin by making amends to ourselves. But how do we do this? I suggest asking the "committee," those voices in our heads that criticize us. In ACA, this is referred to as the Inner Critical Parent. We can apologize to our True Self for the messages we told ourselves and acted on—dysfunctional beliefs and rules we internalized as children.

> *My Bad*
>
> *I know I called you fat, criticized the way*
> *you looked in jeans, particularly from the back.*
> *That roll around your middle—I know it hurt when*
> *I said it was permanent.*
>
> *Your grandmother had that midriff too.*
> *Remember her at 67*
> *in your graduation photo?*
> *You made her dresses in flowered*
> *fabrics to stretch across her middle. Did you*
> *love her less when she was more?*

216

Also, the wrinkles and your saggy neck. It's so damn
tempting for me to focus on the folds, to mourn the taut
tanned flesh you used to flash around. I'm sorry
you feel old, but remember your mother didn't get
to age. Take comfort in the years you got she didn't.

Did I make you take the first job that was offered?
Did I tell you money would compensate for feeling bored
or terrified, or terrified and bored, in equal measure
sometimes all at once? Did you believe me when I said
you'd never succeed without a man to get you clients?
I'm sorry.

I'm sorry for all those men I talked you into falling for.
They were dramatic, yes, flashy smiles and smooth
tongues. I let you fantasize about forever when they were
only good enough. Forgive me. I let you settle.

Those masks I made you wear—the sultry student,
pretty lawyer, good daughter, complacent companion,
know-it-all—I'm sorry I dressed you in disguise.

I told you Saturdays would bring unrelenting suffering
unless you had a project or someplace to go. I told you
that you had no friends, no one to talk to, life an
endless game of show-and-tell and you with nothing
much to show or tell.

I lied. I was afraid to tell the truth. I was afraid you
would leave unless I kept you entertained, running,
judging, always on the move. Don't move.

217

I talked myself into certain behaviors, generally because I felt afraid or thought I wasn't good enough. By giving voice to my Inner Critical Parent, I see that my behaviors were the result of my survival traits. My True Self can recognize that my Inner Critical Parent may have been intending to help me as a child, without understanding the negative effect of those comments. That may help me soften the voice of my Inner Critical Parent today to make room for my Inner Loving Parent.

PROMPT:

1. List all the judgments you make about yourself and then apologize for treating yourself so badly.

2. Notice all the judgments you make about others. Do you ever make these judgments about yourself? Write about another person who do not like and see how many of the judgments could also be made about you.

3. Find a photo of yourself or look into a mirror and stare into your eyes. What do you need to say to yourself? Write a poem or free-write.

Part of the purpose of amends is to uncover our memories of behavior over which we feel remorse and take responsibility for them. I am sometimes surprised to realize my behavior was not totally wrong. It was driven by Character Traits and faulty thinking.

We can also apologize to our Inner Child. The next section addresses what ACA calls "Reparenting" ourselves. If you are uncertain whether you have an Inner Child, or how that differs from the actual child you were, skip over this section. It took me a couple of years in the ACA program before I recognized my Inner Child and her needs. Some in ACA recovery have identified a number of Inner Children at different ages. When I am triggered today by strong feelings of fear, loathing, or shame, it is often because the present-moment event reminds me of a past event. My Inner Child overreacts.

In reparenting, you can listen to your Inner Child's fears and feelings and help them understand they're not in danger now. They are often frozen in the past, a time when they lacked support and unconditional love. They need to hear and trust you will not judge or abandon them. You can speak directly to your Inner Child, using the "You" form to address them. This creates some separation between your Inner Loving Parent and the child and gives you the space to see and hear your Inner Child without becoming flooded by their thoughts and feelings.

One way of making amends to the Inner Child is to measure the loss between what they got in their dysfunctional home and what they would have received in a healthy family. We acknowledge their feelings about not being heard, seen, protected, etc. We listen to them now and apologize for the times we've failed to do so. The following is an amends to my Inner Child written in the voice of my Inner Loving Parent.

Beneath Your Smile

I'm so sorry no one noticed.
When you sucked your thumb,
no one noticed you were scared.
Had I been with you then,
I would have gathered you in my arms
And said "you're safe with me"
I would have said "I love you," even
*   when you were acting up.*

219

I would have seen when you were
trying to be brave, when you were hiding
in your tree-house, when you were all alone
in your room. I would have asked
how you were feeling. I would have
seen beneath your smile.

CONNECTION TO RECOVERY

In the Fourth Step in ACA, we write a detailed inventory of childhood losses, connecting them to Character Traits. I can review this list, or the poems I wrote in that section of this book, and convert those losses into loving words of comfort from my Inner Loving Parent.

PROMPT:

1. Write about the ways in which you felt abandoned emotionally as a child and allow your Inner Loving Parent to notice and apologize for those losses.

2. Measure the loss between what you received from your dysfunctional family and what you would have received from healthy parents. For instance, you may have received shame, blame and neglect. Write about the loss. Choose a specific childhood situation or write about your entire upbringing.

People We Have Manipulated

The following poem uses a method called "self implication," in which the narrator confesses to some thought or act that makes him or her seem less than admirable. In recovery, we learn to release black or white thinking and come to see that we have "our part" not only in resentments but in the daily decisions in life that lead to hurt and pain. Being willing to admit our part helps us to forgive ourselves as well as others. The poem below reveals my fear of being alone and my futile search for a "rescuer." I manipulated my mother's emergency into trying to get relief.

What is Your Emergency?

We'd been out scuba-diving on Miami's coral reef,
the boat bobbing, nausea for those left aboard,
like my mother, fighting sea swells and cancer,
her stomach tied in scar-knots, twisted pain

radiated from her belly like a lasso chokes a calf.
We went to the ER, needing more than morphine.
But pain meds were all that were on offer.
A handsome doctor, young, and ringless was on call,

and God forgive me, I wanted his attention
wanted to escape my single life in Manhattan,
wanted to alleviate my pain, her pain.
I asked to page him, An Emergency, I said.

And he showed up, breathless, interrupted
no doubt from a real emergency, or at least
something he could cure. For us there was no cure.
Brusquely chastised for crying wolf in his ER.

A shot of something, the pain dove down
to sea floor, skittered into a hermit's cave.
Darkness took the pain, cradled it, settled it
like sediment among the fishes and the brine.

He slipped away, no reply to my apology written
from New York. She slipped away one January day,
slipped as easily as into water, to be startled
and amazed by the streaming life below.

CONNECTION TO RECOVERY

This was a highly traumatic time in my life, as I witnessed my mother's illness and feared I'd lose her. I felt guilty when the doctor was mad at me for claiming an emergency, but at the same time latched onto the idea of him being a savior and rescuing me from being alone in New York and afraid of my mother's death. I had one eye on my mother's pain and the other on the handsome doctor. An Inner Loving Parent would have asked me what I was feeling and helped me recognize my fears. She would have comforted me and told me she would not leave me and I would be ok. When moments of fear or loneliness occur today, I can forgive my Inner Child and reparent her with the loving words of an Inner Parent.

PROMPT:

1. Write about any event where you manipulated or used someone to get something you wanted. Implicate yourself. Then forgive yourself.

2. Look at the metaphor of the ocean in the poem. Water can be both beautiful and dangerous. This is a paradox. Meditate until you find an image like this that can help unlock paradoxical feelings in you.

Our Parents

My mother was pretty and charming, intelligent and witty. She tried to control my father's drinking with the only weapon she knew: contempt. Even after they were divorced, she was bitterly disappointed in him.

Arranging to visit him when I came home from college aroused her anger and put me in the middle of an intolerable situation. I learned to treat my dad with contempt too. My major amends to him, made years after his death, was to write a letter in which I apologized for treating him like a failure and a disappointment. I also wrote a letter to my mother, thanking her for preserving our relationship, even though I had left Jehovah's Witnesses.

With the benefit of hindsight and the compassion we learn in program, we can literally "re-frame" or create a new picture of the people from our past. We can remember the slogan that "hurt people hurt people" and come to see what we may have overlooked in our pain. This is the case with my father.

Restore Us

A faded snapshot. My lips a blur,
long blonde curls cascade to frizzles
like wings of hummingbirds.

Was I smiling, standing with him
near my Mustang, in the parking lot
of the Rescue Mission?

What choice but to smile,
dance the one, two, three,
built into muscle memory?

His hat, a shapeless cotton, top squared,
narrow brim above his awkward grin.
His too-short pants from the grab bag.

I'm in a shiny purple maxi-coat,
fashion next to no-fashion, me
next to not-me.

Bring us back: the father who was not-father,
standing with a daughter who's fading,
who for that moment was willing to pretend,

arms entwined in an inner-city parking lot,
that he might someday take her arm
and walk into another picture,
do what fathers are supposed to do.

I can make amends even to those who are dead by writing a letter or by seeing my childhood differently. By writing about real or imagined stories from my parents' past, I see that they too were affected by family dysfunction. By recognizing that my parents did the best they could and were the products of their own upbringing, I can restore our old photos.

PROMPT:

1.Find a family photo with your parents in it and write about it. Imagine what it would say to you today. Allow the photo to speak to you.

2.Think of a time when you felt ill-will toward a parent or caretaker. Whether or not you acted on it, imagine what your True Self would say to the person today.

Our Partner or Spouse

A partner or spouse knows us better than anyone. Somehow, we think this gives us permission to treat them badly, believing they will always forgive us. Sometimes, we get into a relationship for the wrong reasons—fearing to be alone rather than looking for a partner who can be responsible for his or her own emotional life. Years after we wrote the list I refer to in the poem below and had married, I asked my husband why he married me. He said "because you were independent and I knew you wouldn't make too many demands on me." This wasn't on the list! But it shows he recognized a fellow Adult Child.

Reasons

Think of the list we made in that Manhattan restaurant:
Reasons to get married/Reasons not to get married.

Don't think of where it's gone, how those reasons
skittered off like a snowbank melting in the sun

Assume we couldn't know what almost forty years
would bring, the children, pets, laughs and tears

Don't assume I haven't counted all those cups of
morning coffee, the dishes washed, children bathed

Remember that ten years in, I took the name Lissitzyn,
a name I knew would slow me down, force me to spell

Forget the wrinkles and the sags, the words we didn't
say, the letters that we failed to write

Consider that we were bound to find each other, that
fate was waiting to meld our histories to one

Forgive me for believing otherwise, for doubt,
for thinking I could have made a life without you

CONNECTION TO RECOVERY

There is acceptance here, a recognition that I was attracted
to another Adult Child. I also implicate myself in the line
about self sufficiency: "thinking I could have made a life
without you." My husband has always supported my plans
and projects. Sometimes, as a dreamer, I fail to notice that
he has been the steady one, hauling his briefcase to the
same job for thirty years, doing laundry, delivering cups of
coffee.

Our Children

My children today say that I was a wonderful mother, loving and fun, always in their corner. I'm sure part of that is true. I love children and delighted in mine.

But I was also very anxious and career-driven. Even if they don't think I owe them an apology, it's good to review my behavior. I am committed that my controlling behavior, even if benign, stops with me.

1. Dinner must be on the table right at 5pm, even if I have to hustle everybody to the table.
2. You must enunciate the "t" in button. Also cotton and New Britain.
3. Birthday parties must have a theme and be unique. Painting Wishbone doggie masks, making Barbie clothes, treasure hunt at the Mall.
4. Lessons lead to structure, and reveal your gifts: skating, swimming, soccer, tennis, ballroom dancing, hip hop.
5. Family Sundays before the fireplace are required, playing games everybody wins.
6. Prayer shawls for all, also hand-knit sweaters, handmade flags, plates painted at the Claypen.
7. Home requires a dog and several cats.
8. Earn your own way. Don't depend on anyone.
9. A skinny mirror is your most important fashion accessory.
10. How to demonstrate with just a look I know your father's failings.

CONNECTION TO RECOVERY

I know I can fall into my mother's behavior of showing contempt for my father. I often make fun of my children's father for things he does and says. It's not funny. It's actually passive/aggressive, hoping to drum up sympathy for myself. I have no right to enlist them in my resentments against him. When I find myself reaching for the phone to share a funny story at his expense, I put down the phone. When one daughter complains about her dad, I choose not to share that with her sisters.

Failed Relationships

In reviewing step four in A. A. and in Al Anon, we are asked to review where our conduct has been selfish. ACA is less explicit about using the word "selfish," but in the step four worksheets, we are asked to review our conduct both as children and as adults. Fear may cause us to appear selfish. As we review failed relationships, we often see that we participated in their failure, perhaps by unreasonable expectations, perhaps by being attracted to dramatic or alcoholic personalities, perhaps by people pleasing or failing to state our needs.

The following poem reflects my bad behavior with my best friend from college, Joyce. Joyce served me countless meals, took me into her home and loved me. When, years after we were living on different coasts, I visited her, I repaid her hospitality by ignoring her and running off with one of her friends. I'm grateful that today she has forgiven me.

Joyce

When Joyce picked me up at SFO,
Derek was with her, a charmer who
taught drama, grinning from the back seat.

He held a poster, a blow-up
of my campaign photo from when I ran
for law school president.

What did she think would happen next?
Mix chlorine with ammonia. Nature
does the rest.

Did she expect a restrained courtship,
him reading me Shakespeare in her parlor,
us, the Bennett sisters, traipsing through the countryside,
our full-length petticoats catching on the stiles?

Her two-year-old could not compete.
I'd no truck with Legos, clueless to her plight,
my college friend, now married with a child,
everybody else drunk on themselves.

I bought a black lace negligee at Nordstrom.
Decided Derek would appreciate a fashion show.
Dragged myself back to her apartment two days later.
Besotted with the thin lace of infatuation.

On our silent ride back to the airport, I asked her
to forgive me. Too soon.

CONNECTION TO RECOVERY

I am addicted to drama. When Derek showed up with a huge photo of me, I succumbed to excitement. I need to remember to avoid drama. My Inner Child has always been desperate for attention, particularly from men. My Inner Loving Parent can remind her that she does not need male attention to feel ok. She is perfect just as she is. Derek is no longer in my life. I'm glad that Joyce is still a good friend.

PROMPT:

1. Write about any friend from whom you are or were estranged. What behavior of yours contributed to the estrangement, i.e., how did you harm them? How were you similarly harmed as a child? Write a poem about both the impact of your behavior on your friend and the impact of another's similar behavior on you as a child.

2. Write about how your Inner Child affected your behavior. What Character Trait was he or she acting out?

3. Write about how a Loving Parent or Higher Power would view your actions.

When I first filled out the step workbook in ACA, one sheet asked me to name all my relationships—stating what I expected and what I got. I listed only men. When my fellow traveler started to discuss her female relationships, I realized with a jolt that I had many women friends I hadn't thought to list. My women friends in program help me stay steady and on course.

Years ago, a Brazilian boyfriend (married) said to me, "we are responsible for the people we allow to love us." This struck me as wrong. It wasn't my fault if he couldn't resist me. Or was it? Didn't I know what I was doing was wrong? With hindsight, I need to own responsibility for using other people's feelings. Bob, about whom the following poem is written, is an example.

What about Bob

It's the answer to my secret
security question: what is
your favorite movie?

Bill Murray, stalking his shrink
on vacation, worming his way
into the family dinner table.

His fish named Gil worn in a baggie
necklace along for the trip.
What happens to Gil once
he's off the bus, in hot

pursuit of Dr. Martin?
Funny, Bob. Hapless, Bob.
Not my secret Bob, the Bob

I used, abused, the only man
I knew was only good enough
to get me through. And I
let him love me anyway.

I've loved this film for thirty years,
chuckled, cackled, laughed,
at all the funny parts.

Now I see there is no
funny part.

CONNECTION TO RECOVERY

The amends to this man did not go well. I need to remember that sometimes it's unwise to stir up old emotions. When in doubt about a relationship, I can check my motivations. If I am motivated by needing validation or praise, I remember that true self esteem can never come from other people. My Inner Loving Parent reminds me that I don't need the praise of others to change the way I feel about myself.

PROMPT:

1. Write about someone you hung out with or hooked up with because he or she was "good enough."

2. Write about your own sense of being only "good enough" for someone else to love.

3. Think of a film in which there was a character that today reminds you of how you used to be or how you don't want to be. Write about that character. What would that character say to you?

People in Authority We Defied

I quit a job because I got into a tussle with the dean of the university where I was teaching. I had good "reasons" for feeling betrayed, but I also was ego run riot. I wanted to do my job "my way." He wanted me to follow the job description. Today, I am grateful I quit, as it led to my writing career. But I am not proud about the way I quit. I eventually made amends to him. The following poem resulted from a "line prompt," which I explain below. I wrote it from the point of view of the dean, in his voice.

The Dean

It's Thursday noon, another God-damn faculty meeting.
I see a room of bored teachers munching stale cookies,

waiting for this hour to be over, or for a fight to start.
The screen behind me lists the general ed. requirements,

dense black type in columns under headings. Will
fisticuffs break out between Philosophy and Spanish?

They think I have a wife, back at our old school in Kansas.
I made her up. That way, at least I get my weekends free.

I always start each meeting with an academic joke
I find online. They laugh because they have to.

I've never taught a class in blue jeans on the grass
and now I never will. Dress down day means hold the tie.

I wish I could adjourn this meeting and slip out for a beer,
exchange my Volvo for a Porsche, find a girl who likes to flirt.

Perhaps I'd ask if I could sit down, pretend I'm no one
in particular, enjoy her smile, lick the beer foam off her lips.

CONNECTION TO RECOVERY

In writing this poem, I uncovered a human side to the Dean-someone who longed to drink a beer with a pretty girl. I didn't know I would end the poem this way. Writing helps me find compassion for others even when I don't intend to. By writing in his voice, I put myself in the shoes of someone else--always good for my recovery.

PROMPT:

1. Choose a person you dislike. Then write a poem in that person's voice, trying to see life from his or her point of view.

2. Try the line-prompt format below. Write the following about a person you don't like:

the person is performing a task
an image from the task
the character has a secret
something the character always does
something the character never does
the character tells a particular lie
I have always wanted
another image
Now I want
The truth is
What is the character seeing or doing
The truth is

After you have written with this form, revise your work to reveal the parts that are most meaningful to you.

I had a harder time with the Associate Dean, who is still on my "no never" list, someone to whom I can't imagine making amends. But perhaps, someday.

Quitting Time

We are never, ever, ever
getting back together.
I will never, ever, ever
work for you again.

My defiance like a blowfish:
You don't get to tell me
where to put my file drawer,
where my secretary sits,
when to eat my lunch.

I live in the golden bubble
called entitled. My students love me.

I'm the prom queen of the college.
I twirl my skirt, wave red pom-poms.
My jewelry is 14 carat.

My shoes are Ferragamo.
Yours are Birkenstocks.
I'm not impressed by your PhD

But you apparently know something
I have yet to learn. For once my secretary
is sitting exactly where you say,
I know when to eat my lunch.

I now teach in the same university as the Associate Dean. I'm now an adjunct, no longer able to pretend that my title entitles me to special treatment. I see this woman frequently and go out of my way to be pleasant. I don't avoid her or refuse to make eye contact. I know the time will come when I will make amends. In the meantime, I can pray for her.

PROMPT:

1. Write about someone on your eighth step list of people to whom you owe an amends that you feel is a "no never" person. Be as honest as you can about what happened in the relationship.

2. Use the lyrics of a song to write about the relationship. This may help you come at the resentment "slant," as Emily Dickinson said.

REPARENTING YOUR INNER CHILD

As we begin to heal, feelings will return. We will learn to recognize events in our lives that trigger pain or fear from the past. As adults, we berate ourselves with the same critical messages we heard in childhood. Those messages are not "true." They are not even current. They are old, old, old.

Identifying the Voice of the Inner Critical Parent

We learn to separate the voice of the Inner Critical Parent (in AA we call it the "Committee") from our True Self. Many of us suffer from a feeling that we are not good enough, that we did something wrong, or are not deserving of recovery. Although this is often called "low self esteem," I prefer to think of it as the shame that results from a voice in our heads that tells us we are wrong. We need to get the shaming messages down on paper to see them for what they are: messages from the past that need not govern life today. Shaming messages are perfect for a List Poem, as we can generally make the list without much effort.

You Should Have Known Better

What did you think was going to happen?
Haven't I told you before not to—
Will you never learn?
Great. You've done it again.
If I've told you once, I've told you a thousand times—
Busy hands are happy hands—
Don't just stand there. Get moving.
Are you going to wear that?
Can't you get it through that thick head of yours?
You never listen to a thing I say.

I knew you'd mess it up.
You didn't plan your time effectively.
You forgot the most important part.
You're so much prettier when you smile.
Stop singing. Just stop singing.
Why can't you be more like your brother?
Did those pants shrink in the wash?
Don't you remember?
There you go, exaggerating again.
Language, dear. Language.
Don't flatter yourself.
I'm not wasting my money on you.

I am powerless to change the negative messages I give myself until I can first hear them. If I imagine myself saying these things to an actual child, whether as parent, relative, or teacher, I realize the harm they caused me. When I asked other writers to share the messages they heard, I realized I had "forgotten" some of the messages I heard. This is the power of working together in recovery. I can also ask if any of these messages may have been offered in a genuine effort to help me. I remember that my parents passed on messages they may have heard from their parents.

PROMPT:

1.Write all the hurtful things you hear in your head or tell yourself. Notice how they pile up.

2.If you find yourself judging others, write down what you say about them. This, too, is the voice of your Inner Critical Parent. Judging others creates the neural pathways of criticism that can splash back on you.

Finding the Voice of an Inner Loving Parent

Our goal in recovery is to substitute the voice of an Inner Loving Parent for the critical parental voice. At a women's retreat a few years ago, the leader asked half the group to sit in chairs in a circle. The other half stood behind the chairs. Each group was about twenty women. The leader asked each seated woman to whisper what she wanted to hear in childhood to the woman standing behind her. After hearing from the seated woman, each standing woman moved to the chair to her left and repeated this process until she returned to her starting point. The inner and outer circles then reversed positions. Although you might expect that each standing woman heard twenty different messages, the whispered messages were all variations on three themes:

1. *I love you just the way you are.*
2. *I am here for you and will not leave you.*
3. *I want to help you to find the future that you desire.*

Each woman wanted to know that she was loved unconditionally, that her caregiver would not abandon her, and that her caregiver genuinely had her best interests at heart. These sound like such simple messages. But many of us grew up with conditional love, a lack of physical or emotional (or both) safety, feeling abandoned in our violent and dysfunctional homes, and a deep-seated sense that we didn't matter.

AA, Al Anon and ACA all address different aspects of the disease of alcoholism and family dysfunction. But all three programs recognize that the disease of alcoholism results in fractured relationships. We long to be connected, but we lack the skills to develop meaningful relationships. As we recognize that our difficulties stem from behaviors learned in childhood, we realize that we can change those behaviors. We can stop people-pleasing. We can talk about our feelings rather than denying or stuffing them. In short, we can grow into our True Selves. Many of us feared there was no self beneath our survival strategies. Reconnecting with that self and allowing him or her to experience joy is one of the fruits of working a 12-step program.

The first step in reparenting is to find your Inner Child and to let him or her speak. The Inner Child is frequently angry, confused and lonely. They feel they have been abandoned. They need to know that you want to hear their voice.

In AA, Al Anon, and ACA we seek to make "conscious contact" with a Higher Power. In ACA, we also learn to become our own Loving Parent and embody the love and acceptance we longed for as children. Many ACAs believe the Loving Parent is the voice of a Higher Power. We needed to hear loving messages as children and we need to hear them today.

Today, I can write what I want to hear from a loving parent and repeat those words. I have recorded them in my voice so I can listen to them on my phone when I walk. I believe I can change my neural pathways from negative to positive messages. This poem lists some of those loving words:

My Inner Loving Parent Speaks

You are my precious daughter
and I love you just the way you are.
You don't have to wear pretty clothes
or smile or sing for me to love you.

If you don't know how to do something
let me know and I will help you.

There are a lot of things that you are naturally good at--
you are a very good artist and writer
you are very good at playing gently with little animals
and children, you have wonderful imagination.

There are other things that you will need to practice
to get good at, like sports and math.
I can help you learn those things.
Just don't quit when it seems hard.

If someone hurts your feelings
I hope you will come and tell me.
Everyone's feelings get hurt sometimes
that's OK, but if you tell me it won't feel so bad.

I know you sometimes don't understand
why dad can act so mean.
I want you to know that he is sick
and he really can't help it.

We must treat him gently
even though he sometimes does not treat us gently.

It's OK to get angry and
it's OK to be mad
it's not OK to hit your brothers
but it is OK to tell them how you feel
and to also come and tell me.

I will find places for you to have fun
and I will find other children to be your friends.

I want you to not keep secrets
and tell me things even if you think
it might hurt me to know them.

If you aren't sure how to make up
after a fight with someone
come and see me and I will give you some ideas
on how to make it better.

I know sometimes people say things
meaning them to be funny
and they don't feel funny to you.
That's OK.

Sometimes people use telling jokes
or calling names in a way that feels hurtful.
I want you to be able to laugh at funny things
and to know when things are not really funny.

Even though I sometimes get mad at your father
I want you to know that I am not going to leave you.
I will always be here to take care of you and your
brothers and things will be OK.

I want to help you think of what you might like to be
when you grow up.
Any idea you have is OK to explore.
I will be happy to explore them with you.
Let's dream big.

CONNECTION TO RECOVERY

I look for success in program, moments when I tell the truth, engage in a difficult conversation, when I play and have fun or simply take care of myself. I write these moments down in my journal because I have found that I will "forget" them and rob them of their power. Then I adopt the voice of my Inner Loving Parent and say "well done. I'm proud of you." I offer these same words of affirmation to others in program. Modeling the voice of an Inner Loving Parent for others helps both them and me grow into our True Selves.

PROMPT:

1.Picture your ideal loving parent. What qualities does this parent possess? How do they interact with their children? Revisit any wound or loss from your past and write what an loving parent would have said to help you.

2.Think of all the times as a child you were scared, lonely or confused. Write a message from your actual parent or caretaker that would have made your situation better.

3.Think of a recent incident where you felt scared, lonely or confused. Revisit that moment and meet yourself with self-love and compassion.

Listening to Your Inner Child

What does it mean to "Reparent?" Reparenting is a process that involves recognizing when our Inner Child is hurting or acting out and validating their feelings and pain. We can give our Inner Child the validation, reassurance and unconditional love they longed for in childhood. Today we can tell them loving messages they did not hear in childhood, messages like "You're enough" and "It's okay to feel sad (hurt, angry, etc.)," and "You're safe now with me." We talk our Inner Child "off the ledge" when they're feeling sad, scared, angry or ashamed. We help them understand "this is not that," and help them see reality more clearly.

When I am particularly stirred up by someone or something, it's generally because my Inner Child is reacting to a childhood trigger or wound. She doesn't always know she has an Inner Loving Parent to help her through life. As a child, I wanted my father's rants to be over. I wanted my going door-to-door as a Jehovah's Witness to be over. I wanted the pledge of allegiance, which I was not allowed to participate in, to be over. Even today, I will get to an event and immediately think: "How long before I can go home?" Even if I want to be there and like the people, my Inner Child feels off-balance, insecure. She wants assurance from me that I will not make her stay out too late and that I will take her home where she feels safe. Today, I am better at recognizing and honoring this feeling as a trigger from my past. We don't need to run. I can reparent my Inner Child and help her overcome her fears.

I wrote this poem in the voice of my Inner Child when she has been triggered by an event that makes her feel unsafe:

Home

I want to go home.
I don't like it here.
Nobody here is like me.

Home on the range
There's no place like home
Home again. Home again. jiggedy jog.

Home body
Homey. "Will you love me
even when I'm unhappy"

Home is where the heart is.
Home is where you hang your hat.
Somewhere over the rainbow—

Hold hands to cross the street
Hold hands. Hold my hand.
Will you walk me home?

CONNECTION TO RECOVERY
When I entered each of my twelve-step groups for the first time, I was overwhelmed with the feeling: "I'm home. I'm where I am supposed to be." My Inner Child is afraid to open a door when she can't see who or what is inside. I know this stems from the fear and uncertainty of finding the "good dad" or the "bad dad" when I came home as a child. Doors still trigger me, but I can talk my Inner Child through her fear, reminding her that any twelve-step group will be welcoming and safe.

Finding humor in your Inner Child is vital. We often are far too serious, which sometimes makes our Inner Child afraid that she has done something wrong. By being able to laugh at our mistakes and hold childhood memories lightly, we can find the fun or irony in something that seemed painful in childhood. We can "reframe it," as therapists would say. In the dialogue poem below, I talk in my Inner Child's voice to my mother about a nickname I found painful in childhood.

Tinoskaya

You named me Tino. How could you?
   Could what?
Name me with a boy's name.
   We didn't know.
Everybody knows "o" is for boys.
   We thought it was cute.
Like Bagel-head is cute for Peter?
   Well, you must admit, his head does look—
Not funny, mom. Not funny. And, and
I felt dumb when there was a boy at camp
named Tino, and Tino was on his towel,

247

and Tino was on my towel, and—
Did anyone make fun of you?
Well, no. But I was embarrassed, and now I
don't want to take my towel to camp tomorrow.
You don't have to. You can take
a plain towel .
OK. Well. OK. And anyway, I don't like
that camp.
What don't you like?
I don't want to be away from home.
I want to be with you.
And I want to be with you!
Let's plan something fun to do together!

*

Years later, my friend Dolina, tells me she nicknames
all her friends with Russian-sounding endings,
just because it's fun. Today, she names me
Tinoskaya. If I'd never been Tino, I couldn't be
Tinoskaya today. A super cool, fun nickname

CONNECTION TO RECOVERY

By finding humor in my childhood, I can see that
I often took everything too seriously, one of my
Character Traits. I know my parents did not
consciously name me with a boy's nickname. I
have adopted Tino as the name for my Inner
Child, a sign that I love the name.

Another idea is to write from your Inner Loving Parent to your Inner Child as she grew at different ages. Let your child write to your Inner Loving Parent and wait for a response. Allow your Inner Loving Parent to love you and listen to you at each stage. Imagine yourself at six years old and "talk to" yourself in the voice of an Inner Loving Parent. Then have your child progressively grow older, still speaking to the Inner Loving Parent. See what they have to say to each other. This dialogue begins with the Inner Child. The Inner Loving Parent responds. If you'd like, you can play with using your non-dominant hand to write your Inner Child's response. Switch to your dominant hand to write your Loving Parent's dialogue. In the dialogue below, the Inner Child's words are on the left and the Inner Loving Parent responds on the right.

Offerings

Here is a photo of a family at a dining table.
Pork chops and peach pie. They are telling
what they did that day. It's not my family.

　Here is a bunch of buttercups. You can tell
　if you like butter if you hold them under your chin.
　You can also tell if I like you. I do.

Here is the ruffled bathing suit I wear at the pool.
Looks a little babyish, but the pink flowers are cute.
I hope that new boy likes it. Where did he go?

Here is a journal. You can write what you feel
and think. Even the yucky parts. I want to read it.
Maybe that new boy will show up.

Here is the Barbizon Hotel on Lexington Avenue.
I don't belong. On weekends, I should be
having fun in the city, but I'm back at Port Authority.

Here are tickets to Giselle, As You Like It,
and a lecture at the Y. You can go by yourself.
Save a seat for me. I'll be there.

Here are two boxes of ashes.
My mother and father are dead.
Are they done being mad at each other?

Here is a shovel to plant their ashes under a tree.
They aren't mad anymore. They love each other
and they love you.

Here are my three daughters. They are frisky
as kittens. We eat peach pie. We talk about
what we did today. Did you send them to me?

Here is a picture I made of them before they were
born. They each have a piece of you inside.
Aren't their ruffled bathing suits adorable?

CONNECTION TO RECOVERY
I remind myself that I am worthwhile and lovable, then and now. In recovery I can revisit the past and give myself what I needed then. Images from the dialogue helped me discover my True Self. For example, I loved wildflowers as a child. I still do. I loved the theater and ballet. My Inner Loving Parent reaffirms me and says I don't need someone to go with or give me permission to go alone.

For these Prompts, follow the same dialogue approach as I used in the poem above.

1.Imagine yourself at the age of innocence, before you became aware of the need to develop defenses. What did you love to do? What was your favorite color? pet? game? song? Share that with your loving parent or your Higher Power—whatever image you can use that knows you deeply and wants the best for you. What would that person say back to you? Write this as a back-and-forth dialogue.

2.Continue in your dialogue as you age. Share your fears and hopes. Be as specific as you can. What did you first imagine as a career? As a life goal? When did you first develop talents or tastes? What were they?

3.Were there things you could not tell your parents? Tell them to your Inner Loving Parent now.

4.If there were hurts or confusions, share them. Ask your Inner Loving Parent to validate your feelings and help you see other options you may have had.

5.Have you become a parent or taken on a parental role? Share your hopes and dreams for your own children. If you are estranged in some way, tell your Inner Loving Parent what happened. If you have experienced joy, share that too.

6.See what images or objects hold the most resonance in the story of your journey and your dialogue. Give that image or object to your Inner Loving Parent and write down what he or she says back to you.

FINDING YOUR TRUE SELF

Our Inner Child is a part of us that was once fearless and fun-loving, but then developed protections against inconsistent caretakers and a chaotic home. How do we find this child? Find photographs of yourself until you find an age (generally three or four) before you began to adopt defenses. Focus on the light in your eyes, the smile on your face and the delight you experienced in life.

From the Washtub, 1948

I peek out of a washtub on a Christmas card.
"Merry Christmas from Dick, Susie and Christine."
I was not yet one year old, had not discovered the brook,
ice skates, feeding calves or cuddling kittens.

I didn't know that I'd come to love wild flowers—
Queen Anne's lace, lilacs, dandelions.
I hadn't yet picked the first violets of spring,
placed them in a silver vase to surprise my mother.

I didn't know how to read, hadn't yet heard
mama's voice, "There's no place like home."
My blankie was still pristine—blue on one side,
pink on the other. But I was me, washtub me,
naked me, smiling my delight at being cherished.

CONNECTION TO RECOVERY

We were all innocent once. I can recapture that innocence by writing about a photo of me as a baby. I can also see that my parents loved me. They were proud of their new baby and put me on a Christmas card. Finding family photos helps me retrieve happy memories.

252

As we review our childhood, we look for the moment when we turned from a wide-eyed child, trusting and loving, to someone who stifled feelings. We want to recapture the essence of that child. Can we integrate that childlike sense of hope and joy with the adult longing to be known for who we are, to connect with others, to do meaningful work?

In recovery, some of us take a long time to figure out "who we are" without alcohol and the obsession over other people. Sometimes we look back and don't recognize ourselves. This became very clear to me one day when I found a newspaper clipping that I had apparently kept from my college days in Berkeley.

Who Am I ?

I see a student in a newspaper clipping,1969,
yellowed in my drawer. Somebody cut it out.
It must have been me.

She's handing a flower to a boy soldier
with a pointed gun. Maybe it was People's Park.
Perhaps the Third World Liberation strike.

And if it's me, what did I mean, handing him a flower?
Did I mean: "make love, not war,"
or was I just polite? Or maybe funny? Or ironic?

253

These emotions elude me now.
That is, if it was me.

What did he think, this guy whose number had come
up, guarding vacant lots, trying to foil plots
of students who smoked pot, planned to turn the world
far out?

Did he see just a girl, mini-skirt and boots, leather
vest with swinging fringe? She's gone now, that girl,
both of them.

People's Park is a parking lot again. Soldiers don't
get handed flowers. The girls where they've been sent
aren't wearing miniskirts.

CONNECTION TO RECOVERY

I see a certain bravado in this newspaper clipping. I know I
was not as confident as the girl in this picture. I can have
empathy for that girl today. I can also recognize that I was a
perpetual on-looker in a tumultuous political time. I never
took a stand for any cause. I talked myself out of taking any
risks. Today, I can ask myself what is worth fighting for and
take a stand.

PROMPT:

1.Find or imagine a photo of you as a young adult before
recovery. Describe what you are wearing. Wonder what
was going through your mind. Put another person in the
photo (real or imagined) and see how that changes your
piece.

2. Meditate on your hopes and dreams as a young person.
Imagine those dreams coming true and write a profile of
yourself.

Search your name on *Google.* I did this on my birthday one year, and was shocked to find a Christine Beck who had just died. She had been married to a man named Larry, my husband's name. But most bizarre of all, she lived in Spencer, Iowa, a town of 900 people where my dad was raised. The chances of finding a reference on Google to someone who died in Spencer is infinitesimally small. Had I not searched on my birthday, I never would have found this entry. Was this simply a stunning coincidence? Perhaps it was a "God moment." I chose to find a way to relate to this dead woman.

Googling Myself

She pops up on page one – a woman with my name –
Christine Beck – pretty, with a cap of hair like duckling
fluff, from Spencer, Iowa –

a speck-sized town where Grandpa Bob lost his farm,
toiled defeated for the railroad, raised a wagon-load
of misery I called Dad.

A place I haven't been for fifty years, but Christine's been in Spencer
all along, married to a Larry, same as me, watching birds,
watering her garden, face as wide as corn fields in September.

She's been the school librarian, perhaps the one who first
installed the internet, or who enticed the gawky
or the rejects from the team to try on someone else's life.

There are other Christine Becks, but none that live
so far away or strike so close to home. This Christine's
dead, dead at 51, her death published on my birthday, dead

of nothing her mourners care to name. How can I miss
someone I didn't know? Yet here are two Christines,
familiar as rhubarb pie, as close as bodies on a bus.

I imagine a simpler self, one who loved books and helped the students who didn't fit in. As a new lawyer at a huge New York City law firm, I immediately felt I'd made the wrong career choice. I'd gone to law school because a boyfriend was in law school. This was both people-pleasing behavior and a lack of any idea of my True Self. I remember thinking at that law firm desk that I wanted to be a teacher. But I was thinking about teaching law and I lacked the scholarship credentials to do that. Twenty-five years later, I did get a job teaching law – to paralegals. The alternate life of the Christine Beck I found on Google lived in my fantasy small town of Spencer. It has sidewalks, also part of my childhood dream, an image of connection and safety. This is all part of my True Self.

PROMPT:

1.*Google* yourself and write about what you find (or don't find.)

2.Invent *a Google* article that you would like to find about yourself. Add accomplishments, family, where you lived. Make up a life consistent with your True Self!

I continued practicing law for twenty-five years. There were definite advantages, such as a good salary and the ability to work part-time while we raised our three daughters. But being a lawyer was a mask I wore, a mask of respectability and professionalism. Inside, I was still an Adult Child. Here is another poem where I reveal all the masks I have worn over the years.

Can You See Me Now?

First, there were the Lennon Sisters.
I was Janet, singing "Que Sera,
Sera, whatever will be will be,
the future's not ours to see."

Janet, in her tight-waisted dress,
twirling in her crinolines and tulle,
perpetually young and pretty,
bubbles wafting behind her.

Can you see me?

Line leader, answer-ready,
at least to questions that had answers—
give this girl a pencil and watch her write
a 4th grade winning essay, read aloud

on the radio, classmates clustered envious
as my words accompanied a classical piece:
"It sounds like fairies dancing in the snow."
That's what I said. That was when I believed

in fairies. Then I skipped a grade—half
fourth, half fifth, always in between,
playing catch-up or not enough.
Addition required counting on my fingers.

Chosen last for sports, accused of stealing
milk money, flailing at the ball, converted
to a cult, no flag salute, no birthdays,
Christmas, mask of religious righteousness.

Can you see me now?

Pappagallo flats, tiny bows
cut-out to show a peep of toe.
Liberty of London blouses. My outer layer
said Princeton. My underwear said
Lawrenceville.

The Berkeley mask required army surplus
stores and marijuana, long hair and short
skirts, drama class without a call-back,
college boys, each one Mr. Right.

The lawyer mask suited my superiority,
entitled to give advice, *Brooks Brothers* suits,
Ferragamo shoes, *Coach* briefcase. I knew
the first day on the job I wouldn't last.

Can you see me now?

Eventually *Talbots* wife, *Volvo* carpool, three daughters,
the life of little girls eclipsed my past, dressed
in matching dresses like the Lennon sisters.
We blew bubbles in the park.

I grew into my masks, until they hardened into stone,
then began to crack.

I can still wear masks to disguise my True Self. What are those masks today? One of my masks is "leader" in recovery.

When I check my motivations (am I seeking praise? am I trying to get people to like me? am I controlling because I am afraid of chaos?) I can step back and resume my True Self as a member in recovery.

PROMPT:

1.Write a poem about all the masks you have worn in life to disguise your True Self. You may not have recognized them as masks in the past, but think of any time you tried to present yourself as something you knew you weren't. Try to incorporate specific details, as I do above, of what you wore, or said, or thought, what you compared yourself to on TV or in books.

2.What mask do you still wear at times? Write about your fears of letting go of your mask.

3.Write about who you would be if you could drop your mask and be your True Self.

LEARNING HOW TO PLAY AND HAVE FUN

Before recovery, I hated weekends. During the work-week, I knew what was expected of me and I knew how to do it. The hours were filled with projects. On the weekends, I had to consider what to do with free time. What would make me happy?

The prospect of free time terrified me. I was filled with anxiety. How do I "account" for using my free time wisely? As a lawyer, I accounted for my time in six- minute increments on a "timesheet," used for billing clients. Who was keeping my timesheet on the weekends? ME

I did not know how to play and have fun. This is one of the promises of ACA and although it may sound frivolous compared with discovering my True Self, it is actually a touchstone to my True Self. What makes me happy? When do I feel joy?

Joy, at least for me, feels like an outlook on life, one that insists in your soul that "everything is ok" even when all evidence seems to point in the opposite direction. I ask myself, "Am I fulfilled and flourishing?" If I can answer "yes" even when my kids are fighting, or I get a rejection notice, or notice another wrinkle on my neck, I feel joy. What makes me come alive? Sure, sometimes it's floating in the waves in the Bahamas, but more often, it is the feeling of human connection, some sense of the profound. It's the feeling we explored when we wrote about spiritual experiences.

My granddaughter is a perfect object lesson. When she was two years old, the world revolved around her. She hadn't learned to put on her defenses yet. How would she approach the world? What would she say about her life? I tried to write in her voice:

Jumping for Joy

I'm jumping on a trampoline with my best friend Florence Mae. I am wearing my blue Cinderella dress it's satin with sequins and see-through parts Florence Mae has on a princess dress too. Hers is purple. We jump up and down first one then the other the wind flips up our hair we're laughing in the breeze

I'm having dinner at a restaurant with Grammy who bought me a strawberry milkshake to drink along with my dinner. Usually a strawberry milkshake is a special treat or a dessert but I love it with my dinner Grammy is the best

I'm jumping from a chair to my couch my favorite way to jump is to just fall forward and know the couch will catch me so far it always catches me and this is really fun the grown-ups sometimes get scared but I'm not scared one bit

I like to sing at the piano I like to make a really loud song and then the grown-ups think it's funny I don't know that I'm not much of a singer but that doesn't matter yet

I have Butterfly wings and I run up and down the hall saying zoom zoom zoom and mommy takes my picture saying zoom zoom zoom and then she sends the video to Grammy and Grammy really likes seeing me say zoom zoom zoom and then she sends the video to her friend and her friend really likes it too when I say zoom zoom zoom butterfly wings are the best

The best kind of party is a cupcake party with my friends and strawberry cupcakes then we get to put on frosting and sprinkles sometimes whipped cream too my favorite sprinkles are the pink and blue ones also the yellow and purple purple is my favorite

My mommy cuddles me at bedtime and reads me stories sometimes I read them to her she is the best mommy ever   one time she went on a trip to her friend named Big Elizabeth and I was sad   I remembered the song Grownups Come Back and at bedtime daddy gave me a picture of mommy to go to sleep with when my mommy came back I told her I missed her and I loved her

Even if I can't remember playing as a child the way my granddaughter does, I know that she is an ordinary child and so was I. Being silly and laughing at myself is one way I can lighten up. I share photos of my granddaughter's antics with others in recovery because it lets us connect and laugh. At the end of ACA meetings, each member says an affirmation. Mine is frequently "I will lighten up," or "I will wear life like a loose garment." A sponsee wrote this phrase on a birthday card to me, so I know I must be saying it often!

PROMPT:

1.Imagine yourself at two years old. Write without concern over word choice or punctuation about the things you did that made you happy.

2.If you cannot access your own emotions, find another two-year-old. I attend a meeting in a church with a nursery school. Once I observed three-year-old's marching down the hallway cheering for a sports team I'd never heard of. I'm guessing they hadn't either. But they cheered as if those cheers would win the game. It's like that. Find that moment.

FINDING SERENITY, PEACE, AND LOVE.

How do we find peace? How do we integrate those painful childhood memories with our lives today and accept what cannot be changed, without blame or resentment? I deeply resented being a Jehovah's Witness and having to convert people. As you can see below, I found peace in the natural world.

Field Service

In my teenage years,
instead of shopping at the mall,
I spent my Saturdays
selling leaflets door to door.

My mission was to announce
the coming war of Armageddon,
when everyone who wasn't saved
would face a fiery death.

We called it Field Service.
I recall those years one Sunday
in Vermont, as I embark
down a meandering country lane.

I find a field of green alfalfa. It grows
beneath a row of pines that seem to guard
the tender shoots like ministers or wise men.

Nearby an ancient graveyard lies locked
behind a picket fence, festooned
with Black-eyed Susans, the headstones
smoothed by weather and the years.

I rest beneath of the comfort of the trees,
breathe in the incense of the fields,
where no one knows if you are saved or damned.
Amid the harmony of growing things,
I plant my past beneath the earth
and sing the praise of pines.

CONNECTION TO RECOVERY

I can let nature remind me that I am whole and healed. Trees can protect me. I can let go of my resentment over being a Jehovah's Witness and allow myself to be a different kind of "minister" today, neither proselytizing or evangelizing, but standing witness to the recovery of others and holding their stories as they heal.

PROMPT:

1. Write a poem about your "religion" as a child if you had one, or your lack if you did not. Compare it with your concept of spirituality and a Higher Power today. What aspects of old thinking can you "plant" and let go?

2.How do you find serenity in the midst of a challenge? Write about the struggle and how it feels when you can let go.

We all want love. We wanted the love of our parents. We want the love of our fellows. Many of us find an intimate partner in life. Some do not. In the following poem, I recognize the love I felt for the husband of a dear friend. I didn't call it love at the time, but I see now that I trusted him with my life and experienced a moment of joy and exhilaration that I will recall forever.

The man I wrote about was a physicist. He spent his career writing mathematical hypotheses about subatomic particles and testing them. But when he came home from the lab, he loved to ride his motorcycle and have fun. He learned to fly a glider and asked if I wanted a ride. Something about the freedom of being up in the silent air with this man led me to this poem about love.

Flying with the Man Who Looks at Nothing

The man who looks at nothing eyes the universe,
twists a shock of hair as he considers probability,
what is there, what could be, hypotheses

requiring massive hunks of metal apparatus
to hurl neutrinos, quarks, particles that might set off a spark,
a release of energy, the kind that shifts between a woman,

say, lined up for a mocha latte on a Tuesday workday
and the man who jostles her, confronts a hunger
she didn't know was eating at her. Then,

the man who looks at nothing stops twirling,
as if the curl relaxing on his shoulder could shift the laws
that govern speed, or depth, or sound, the certainty

we reach for flailing out our arms at night,
when there's maybe someone, or not someone,
but nothing we can hold or get our minds around.

This afternoon, we're in a glider, looking down at trees

265

that hide my street, a street that seemed so solid, straight,
its lights perched on neat poles, sidewalks, white center lines,
covered up with what appears to be a canopy of green.

I'm flying with a man who's floating free, released this
afternoon from formulas, experiments, just the swish of wind
we cannot see.

We're held up by improbability. We dip and lift without
propeller, engine, no metal, no apparatus.
The man who looks at nothing is invisible to those below.

And it's enough today to sense an inkling of an energy,
a spark of something others look for daily,
but fail to find, just as tomorrow, back at the blackboard,

in the lab, turning on the cyclotron, he'll miss again what
he's not looking at, elusive as a curl of hair,
its sigh before the pull of gravity.

CONNECTION TO RECOVERY

Love is available to me. As I learn to trust and become vulnerable, I can experience the joy and inspiration that I used to believe was reserved for an intimate partner. I can recognize codependency in my life—where am I looking for love, affirmation and attention from people who cannot provide it? I can seek instead the love, affirmation and attention of my Inner Loving Parent and those in recovery who can be truly emotionally available to me.

PROMPT:

1.Write about a time of romantic longing in your life. It may be a first love or a more recent one. It may be a fictional character you invent.
2.Allow yourself to feel connected in some unusual way (such as in the glider above.)

WRITING YOUR WAY INTO THE FUTURE

Experiment with writing your own obituary. This may sound grim, but imagine the person you want to grow into and then put him or her on paper. As I create my True Self, I celebrate her accomplishments as a person in recovery.

Gone Gently

Christine would have appreciated this title. She loved literature, particularly poetry. She'd love to see Dylan Thomas upended. Instead of "do not go gently into that good night," she did go gently, for she lived a full, fascinating life and at her end had no regrets.

Christine was raised in New Jersey by parents who married too young, died too young, and loved each other and her imperfectly. Yet they set her on a path to love language, telling dreams over the kitchen table, or listening to Dorothy and Dick Kilgallen on the radio at breakfast. From her mother, she learned to love vibrant fashion, needlework, and little children. She also learned a deep spiritual longing, which took a different path from her mother's, but which still connected them. From her father, she learned a sense of humor and a love of puppies and kittens. Also a love of words, stemming from the spelling bee he won with the word raspberry.

Christine began her career as a lawyer, which didn't suit. She liked telling people what to do and making money, but her heart wasn't in corporate law. She loved teaching adult women law. When she turned 60, they gave her a birthday party with thank you notes she regularly re-read and reveled in.

Had she not begun to drink too much when she turned 50, she would never have discovered that she was an alcoholic, just like her dad. That led to 12-step recovery, which led her to her authentic self and a calling in teaching others in recovery to use creative writing to heal from broken childhoods.

Christine and her husband Lawrence had three daughters and spent their happiest years together raising little children. She got a second bite at the apple with her grandchildren, who truly kept her young.

Her favorite saying to the many women she sponsored in recovery was "wear life like a loose garment."

CONNECTION TO RECOVERY

I can re-invent myself by discovering my gifts and talents and living into them. This is the enactment of Step Twelve— I live my spiritual awakening and share recovery with others. There is no higher calling.

PROMPT:

1.Write your obituary. Use your own voice. Make up accomplishments if you wish. Notice what became important to you in your life.

A BLESSING

I offer each of you a blessing as you write and share your stories. The spiritual gifts of writing for recovery are profound. May you learn to trust your Higher Power to guide your pen, allowing you to find what you need to discover just exactly when you will be able to use that insight for recovery. May you uncover feelings of grief and loss but also of joy and wellness. Know that your writing is perfect and need not be compared with anyone else's.

Learn to share your story and be the power of listening for the story of others. Connect with the community of searchers, who long for family and healing. Remember that recovery, unlike resources in the material world, is limitless and magic. Sharing our recovery expands what is available for others. This is a miracle. I hope your writing for recovery leads you to this blessed place.

Tell me what you think of this book. You can contact me through my website: www:ChristineBeck.net.

APPENDICES

Poetry Terms and How to Use Them

1. Narrative. Telling a story with characters the writer and reader care about. In poetry, unlike much of fiction, we often tell a broken narrative or present just a "narrative thread." This invites the reader to imagine what has been left out of the story and to connect the emotions to experience.

2. Arc and form. Moving back and forward in time. Using "jump cuts" over time. Working to create energy and tension with an ultimate resolution of some kind.

3. Sensory description. Using all five senses (how things look, taste, sound, smell or feel) to be as particular and concise as possible in creating character, scene or image.

4. Repetition. Repetition is a tool that is valued in poetry and often viewed as something to be avoided in other creative writing. The reader enjoys encountering the same word or phrase, rather as we love a refrain in a song.

5. Wordplay. I love a startling word, one that asks me to compare things that are not alike and find the commonality. I also love a "neologism," which is an invented word. Poets get to do this. I made up the word "brazenhood" for a stage of my youth when I drank in bars. I also made up "keekowah" as a birdcall because of its sound.

6. Rhyme. I tend to avoid "end rhyme," rhyming words that occur at the end of lines, because I'm not good at it. I find myself either sounding like "Hop on Pop," or I chose a "forced rhyme," a word that isn't exactly right but is good enough just to get it to rhyme. Then I get distracted trying to find a better rhyming word. Then I've lost my creative impulse and start judging my work. We want to avoid judgment wherever possible. We have been judged and have judged others all our lives. It doesn't work. So when you find yourself saying "this is no good. This isn't working," return to the free-write strategy

and surrender the form you are trying to force your writing to obey. I will often return to a poem and substitute words inside a line that rhyme with a word somewhere else (called "internal rhyme"). This sets up an expectation in the reader that something fun will show up when the reader least expects it.

7. Line endings and stanzas. Poetry is unique in that the writer makes a conscious choice where to end a line and when to begin a new stanza. A line can end where you would put a period, a comma, or take a breath. Or not. If you break the line in a way that doesn't follow the end of a thought, it's called enjambment. (The end of one line is literally jammed into the following line.) Why might you do this? It might create a different meaning to read line 1 as ending with one word and then see what it means when you add line 2. It might be for dramatic effect. It might be to annoy you. It might be to ramp up the energy of the poem. The reasons vary, but the tool is there for the poet to play with. Similarly, not all stanzas must be the same number of lines or begin at the left margin. The key as a writer is to convince the reader that you made your choice for an artistic reason, not that it was random or you were sloppy.

8. Metaphor. Most powerful poems, ones you remember and want to re-read, contain a metaphor that reminds you of your own life. That's one difference between poetry and fiction. I may enjoy a detective story, but finding out "who did it" is a game. I don't re-read it because once I know who did it, what's the point? Yet poetry, good poetry, speaks over time and means different things to different people. In the poem, "The Scarf," yarn is a metaphor--an object that stands for a concept—in this case a family story. As it applies to the entire poem, it is called a "Controlling Metaphor." A metaphor is an object or image that stands for something unlike it. For example, when Emily Dickinson says, "Hope is a thing with feathers," she is comparing a bird to hope. Be aware of metaphor as you write. Be on the lookout for people, places and things that can stand for an idea or feeling.

9. Form. "Form" refers to lines governed by rules involving stress and meter (like iambic pentameter), rhyme or repetition. The most

271

familiar form is the sonnet, which was one of Shakespeare's favorites. I confess that the only poetic form that works well for me is the Pantoum, a form of 4 line stanzas in which the second and fourth lines of one stanza are repeated as the first and third lines of the next stanza. If this explanation makes your eyes glaze over, ignore it. Form isn't important unless it helps you say what you want to say. Remember I said earlier that I love repetition? This is a repeating form, so it uses that tool. It also forces the writer to change the method of writing from a straight narrative, such as "I did this, then I did that" or "I said this, then he said that" to a form of syntax that must rely fully on the line. If you feel stuck in telling too much "story" and not enough reflection in your writing, a form such as this one can really help. So, if writing sonnets helps you unlock your thoughts and connect to your Higher Power, write them. If it doesn't, that's fine too.

11. Turn. A turn is where a poem changes tone, topic, or style toward the end. The sonnet form is designed to turn in the last 4 lines of the 16-line form. Read Shakespeare's sonnet that begins, "My mistress eyes are nothing like the sun." You will see that he turns from insulting her features to praising her at the end of the poem. In "Those Winter Sundays," by Robert Hayden, a son is remembering how his father got him up and ready for church on cold winter mornings. After describing the scene, he turns to a different tone: "What did I know? What did I know? Of love's austere and lonely offices." This is an example of a turn in tone to regret and in style of speech to repetition and more formal diction. Often we surprise ourselves at the end of a poem when we discover that we have written a "turn" without intending to.

12. Found Poems. A found poem is composed from lines you mix and match from any published source. It could be a newspaper article, a letter, the dictionary. Here is a found poem from lines that each writer in my Recovery Writer group wrote in the prompt about masks:

Masks

I kept my "I'm not drunk mask,"
next to my "I wasn't that bad" mask.

Something is wrong! My happy mask
doesn't fit.

I felt my fist fit in her flesh.
"I was old before I was born" mask.

My "class clown mask," when I
was nicknamed Marilyn

Donned my "she's a brain mask"
at college.

In the auditions for "Masks Forever," I
auditioned for love.

Why do I always have to be the boy?
I wailed. I've got my "miserable one"
mask.

We figured it out, each year, with
our "own bottle" masks.

A List of Feeling Words

You can use these to create or discover tone in your writing. You can also use them to put emotion into writing that may seem flat. Finally, you can use these feelings in the Prompt "If Feelings Could Talk."

Abandoned	*Light-hearted*
Appreciated	*Lonely*
Betrayed	*Loved*
Bitter	*Overwhelmed*
Calm	*Regretful*
Confident	*Rejected*
Content	*Relaxed*
Defensive	*Scared*
Depressed	*Spontaneous*
Devastated	*Thrilled*
Diminished	*Tired*
Empowered	*Trusted*
Friendly	*Vulnerable*
Grateful	*Warm*
Helpless	*Humiliated*
Inspired	*Worthless*

Working with this Book in a Group

You can choose to work with the prompts in this book by yourself or in a group. You can jump around and write to sections that appeal to you, wherever you are in the Steps and recovery.

Here are some suggestions on working with this book in a group. Use whatever works for you if working individually. Even if you work individually, I encourage you to share your writing with someone else in recovery. Writing our stories helps reveal buried memories and truths. Sharing our stories helps us heal.

When I work with this book with my writing groups, we start with a "Set Aside Prayer." In order to clear the space for a Higher Power to guide our pen into a place of compassion and healing, we first take the concerns of the day and particularly our concern that our writing will not be "good enough" and set them aside. If you are not working in a group, I invite you to take a deep breath and release all your considerations about your writing: whether it will be grammatically correct, what others might think of it, whether it might be published. The set aside prayer goes something like this:

> God, help me set aside everything I think I know about writing, about how writing can help recovery. Help me set aside all my judgments about my writing and my fears that others may judge me. Help me set aside all the other things I think I should be doing. Remind me that there is nowhere else I need to be and nothing else I need to be doing, so that I can have an open mind and heart today to do the work of writing for recovery.

If you aren't sure about the "God" part, pray to the spirit of creativity within you. The point is to quiet the chatter in your head.

Next, do a "free-write." A free-write is a stream of consciousness writing meant as a warm up. You write whatever pops into your mind without trying to guide the writing in a particular way. Images, phrases, and words will occur naturally in a free-write that you may later use. Start writing and keep at it without stopping for 3-5 minutes. If you are ever stuck for a topic, just write down all the things that are

275

cluttering up your mind. Often, the last thing you write, when you are really pushing to get to the end of the page, will be the most profound.

Don't worry about "telling the truth" or whether what you are writing is "true." If it comes from your subconscious, guided by your Higher Power, it will be emotionally true, even if the particular place, person or thing seems unfamiliar to you. Here are some free-write ideas I have used.

All the things you are afraid of.

Take the word "home" and describe it using words for each of the 5 senses (sight, smell, touch, taste, sound)

All the people who are creating stress in your life.

Words you think of when you hear "vacation" [you can substitute any emotionally-laden word for vacation: marriage, death, school, sex, surprise, birthday, etc.]

Things you are absolutely sure are true.
Things you are absolutely sure are NOT true.
Things you are an expert at.
Things you are absolutely NOT an expert at.
Things that have surprised you.
Names of all the games you can think of.
Names of everyone you know.

Write to a "Prompt"

Then read one of the poems in this book and take twenty minutes (or more) to write a poem, a story, a dialogue, anything that "responds" to that poem. You will see I have a number of specific suggestions beneath each poem, or you can make up your own. These poems are designed to be repeated. Take them in any order that feels right to you.

Connect your Writing to Recovery.

In my writers groups, we gather and read our work, complimenting what works well and reflecting on how the work supports our healing and recovery. If you are working by yourself, write in your journal what you have discovered in your writing that feels important for your recovery today. You may find that your writing shows a new compassion for yourself or for another. You may find it uncovers memories. You may discover a sense of humor you didn't know you had. Perhaps you will discover a connection to one of the steps, such as feeling powerless or searching for connection to a Higher Power.

Some Well-Known Poems to Read.

These may give you inspiration as you write for your recovery. Most of them are readily available online. Check www.poetryfoundation.org.

A Rant, Frank O'Hara. A good example of a rant.

Abandoned Farmhouse, by Ted Kooser. This poem lets the farmhouse tell what happened to the missing people, victims of bad luck and loss. It's a poignant portrait of abandonment.

Daddy, by Sylvia Plath. This rant against a father is filled with rage. She calls him a Nazi. The poem ends, "Daddy, daddy, you bastard, I'm through." It's an excellent anger poem.

Design, Robert Frost. The poem shows a moth trapped by a spider and questions a Higher Power that would design such cruelty. It invites us to contemplate the natural world and the nature of God.

Digging, Seamus Heaney. The power of our ancestors in our lives.

Dragonflies Mating, Robert Haas. This poem contains a chilling portrait of a drunk mother lurching her way through her son's basketball court to pick him up. The son wants to kill her.

Diving into the Wreck, Adrienne Rich. The poem addresses finding the self through the metaphor of exploring an underwater wreck.

Do Not Go Gentle Into That Good Night, by Dylan Thomas. This is a pantoum. I refer to it in my poem "Gone Gently."

Falling in Love is Like Owning a Dog, by Taylor Mali.

Filling Station, Elizabeth Bishop. Bishop, who struggled with depression and alcoholism all her life, writes in this poem "somebody loves us all." Sadly, she could not hold onto this belief.

278

Gathering the Bones Together, Gregory Orr. Orr explores the central trauma of his life, when at age 12 he accidentally shot and killed his brother

God's Grandeur, by Gerard Manley Hopkins. This poem, written by a priest in 1917, shows God through nature. It's beautiful.

Having a Coke with You, Frank O'Hara. A love poem, where love is found in the ordinary moment.

Head, Heart. Lydia Davis. Davis presents the classic dilemma of those new to recovery—how to get from our heads into our hearts.

How It Will Happen, When, by Dorianne Laux. The recognition that a parent is dead.

I Go Back to 1937, by Sharon Olds. The narrator imagines preventing her parents from their disastrous marriage, but then sees the gift that she can write about it.

It All Comes Back, by Galway Kinnell. A father laughs when his little boy sits on his birthday cake by accident, thus rupturing the trust of a child.

Let Evening Come, by Jane Kenyon. "God does not leave us comfortless/so let evening come." This poem offers hope and care from a Higher Power

Marks, Linda Pastan. Getting marks for being a mother. A funny poem that helps us hold life lightly.

My Papa's Waltz, by Theodore Roethke. A small boy clings to his drunken father's shirt, wanting their waltz to continue. This poem expresses the yearning for love from an alcoholic parent.

One Art, Elizabeth Bishop. "The art of losing isn't hard to master."

Sonnet 29, by Shakespeare. This sonnet begins, "When in disgrace with fortune and men's eyes" and continues in a "victim" mode. Then it turns to "haply I think on thee" and everything changes. Although it can be read as a love poem, it can just as easily be about turning our thoughts over to a Higher Power. My favorite poem!

*Stop all the clocks, cut off the telep*hone, W. H. Auden. Mourning the dead.

The Pond, Mary Oliver. "Soon, now I'll turn for home./And who knows, maybe I'll be singing." Oliver is well-known as a poet who finds solace and the spiritual in the natural world.

The Tavern, by Rumi. This 13th century Persian poet talks about the power of alcohol and its effect on the soul. "Whoever brought me here will have to take me home."

This Is Just To Say, William Carlos Williams. An apology for eating plums out of the refrigerator, which is not really an apology but an excuse. It's a "yes-but" amends.

Those Winter Sundays, by Robert Hayden. A child realizes with regret as an adult that his father loved him. It's a touching form of amends.

Wait, by Galway Kinnell. Kinnell is talking to a heartbroken adolescent student about the moment when life will become "interesting" again. It reminds me that pain and grief will pass.

Washing the Elephant, by Barbara Ras. This poem ranges from questions about heaven to an acknowledgement of the power of memory. "It's always the heart that wants to wash the elephant."

What Lips My lips have Kissed, and Where, and Why, Edna St. Vincent Millay. Regret for loves lost.

Won't You Celebrate with Me? by Lucille Clifton. The poem ends with the chilling lines: . . .come celebrate/with me that everyday/something has tried to kill me/and has failed."

Acknowledgements

Thanks to all my friends both in and outside recovery who have helped me write this book. In particular, thanks to my Recovery Writers group, to my poetry group, Partners in Poetry, to Bonnie M. for helpful editorial comments, and to Tony Fusco. Finally, thanks to my family, who have supported and loved me throughout my journey in recovery.

Grateful acknowledgement is made to the following publications in which some of the poems in this book first appeared, sometimes in earlier versions:

Austin Poetry Festival, *Meditation from my Front Step*

Blinding Light, Christine Beck, Grayson Press: *Against the Odds, Swans and Hearts, Portrait in Elizabeth Park, Valley of Shadows*

Caduceus, Yale School of Art, *Grandfather Clock*

Encore, National Federation of State Poetry Societies, *Walking Home*

I'm Dating Myself, Christine Beck, Dancing Girl Press, *Flying with the Man Who Looks at Nothing*

J Journal, John Jay School of Criminal Justice, *If I Should Disappear*

Naugatuck River Review, *Two Figures in Search of a Story*

Passenger, *The Manicure*

Rosebud, *Field Service*

Recovery, *John Doe 43*

Stirred, Not Shaken, Christine Beck, Five Oaks Press: *Take It*

Christine Beck is a poet, teacher, and a member of Alcoholics Anonymous, Al Anon, and Adult Children of Alcoholics. After a twenty-year career as a lawyer, she received a Masters of Creative Writing and now teaches writing and literature as an instructor at the college level. Christine Beck directs a monthly poetry series for the Connecticut Poetry Society at local libraries. She is a former Poet Laureate of West Hartford, CT. Her books of poetry include *Blinding Light*, Grayson Press, *I'm Dating Myself*, Dancing Girl Press, and *Stirred, not Shaken*, Five Oaks Press. She publishes regularly on the website I Love Recovery Café and www.IntheRooms as well as on www.medium.com. Her website is www.ChristineBeck.net.

Printed in Great Britain
by Amazon

79848593R00173